Y0-DOK-935

CONNECTING
SKILLS WORKBOOK

Sherod Miller, Ph. D.
Daniel B. Wackman, Ph. D.
Elam W. Nunnally, Ph. D.
Phyllis A. Miller, Ph. D.

Copyright © 1989 by Interpersonal Communication Programs, Inc.

All rights reserved. No part of this work may be reproduced in any form without permission in writing from the publisher.

Printed in the United States of America.
10 9 8 7 6 5 4 3 2

ISBN-0-917340-16-7

Design: Robert Friederichsen
Typesetting Assistance: Robert Bolenbaucher and Ed Nies

**INTERPERSONAL
COMMUNICATION
PROGRAMS, INC.**
7201 South Broadway
Littleton, CO 80122
Phone: (303) 794-1764

CONTENTS

INTRODUCTION

Life unfolds in a network of relationships. From day-to-day we participate in a variety of interpersonal dances — connections and disconnections — ranging from painful, distressing, and destructive encounters to joyful, meaningful, and productive experiences. Your communication, both verbal and nonverbal, is the "stuff" that initiates, builds, maintains, and destroys relationships. Your words and actions together become both a *vehicle* for relating and an *index* for understanding the nature and quality of your relationships.

Our research and experience indicate that the ingredients of effective communication — those that lead to satisfying and meaningful relationships — flow out of active respect for and accurate awareness of yourself and the other people with whom you interact. How well you communicate your awareness with friends, partner, family members, and people at work determines to a large extent how happy, satisfying, and productive your life is.

The Purpose of This Workbook

As the title indicates, our interest is in helping people learn to connect and disconnect more effectively and satisfactorily — to "win" *inter*dependently rather than to "win or lose" independently.

To accomplish this end, the CONNECTING SKILLS WORKBOOK is designed *to equip you with a set of interrelated communication/ relationship maps and skills*. These maps and skills help you to "learn how to learn" from your day-to-day exchanges and enable you to enhance your relationships. In the CONNECTING SKILLS WORKBOOK your own social networks and current issues provide the examples for learning and practicing communication skills.

Copyright © 1989, Interpersonal Communication Programs, Inc., Littleton, CO

The CONNECTING SKILLS WORKBOOK will help you apply and practice the concepts and skills detailed in its companion text, CONNECTING WITH SELF AND OTHERS.

How You Can Benefit From This WORKBOOK

The maps and skills presented in the text CONNECTING and the worksheets in this WORKBOOK grow out of the rich tradition of communication/interaction analysis and modern systems theory. As such they provide you with a practical integration of theory and methods for understanding relationships and enriching the way you communicate. The WORKBOOK material is designed to increase your:

- *Awareness* of self, others, and your relationships.
- *Skills* for sending and receiving messages more clearly and accurately.
- *Options* for building relationships with friends, family, and work-career associates.

For a more detailed listing of benefits — specific skills and processes which you can acquire or improve — scan the items in the "Communication/Relationship Questionnaire" on pages 14 - 16 in the Pre-Assessment Section. (Notice that the numbers immediately under each item guide you to the chapters in CONNECTING which relate to learning that particular skill or process.) The Pre-Assessment Questionnaire and others throughout the WORKBOOK will help you tailor your "people-skills learning" to your own particular needs.

Stages of Skills Learning

You may find that you go through four distinct stages as you learn the skills in this workbook.

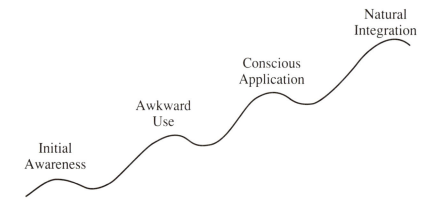

Copyright © 1989, Interpersonal Communication Programs, Inc., Littleton, CO

Initial Awareness. As you become aware of the new frameworks and skills, you will begin to see situations and hear conversations differently. You will notice different ways of relating and communicating than you typically use. You may find yourself in an exchange and suddenly realize how talking differently could help the exchange. If, to alter the interactions, you do not make use of a skill of which you are now aware, do not be discouraged. Rather than putting yourself down for having missed an opportunity to enhance the moment, take satisfaction in the fact that you recognized that there is an alternative. *Being aware of different possibilities is the first step toward communicating in new ways.* At this stage it is typical to feel excited about new possibilities and disappointment with your "failure" to act differently.

Awkward Use. As your awareness of alternatives and the desire to try new ways of relating and communicating increase, you will experience some immediate successes and positive payoffs from your experimenting with the new skills. This will be exhilarating. However, other times things will not go so well. Whether skill use backfires or not, it is normal to feel clumsy and mechanical — not like your real self. Occasionally, someone may poke fun at you, test your resolve, or subtly discourage your change. Others will respond positively. Seek out people who are encouraging.

At this stage you may be tempted say, "It's not worth it" and give up practicing the skills. Also during this stage, your spontaneity lessens. You may feel constrained by the learning process. (Some people say they find it useful to rant and rave about the skills to get the frustration of learning them off their chest.) In any event, keep trying.

Conscious Application. Now you begin to use the skills more effectively, but you are still self-conscious when you use them. You feel more comfortable, and begin to enjoy the results of your changes. You begin to use your own language more in carrying out the skills. Nevertheless, you still have some sense that, "This isn't fully me." At this stage, when you are suddenly aware of having missed a chance to connect with someone better, you also have greater confidence that you are equipped to go back and right the situation.

Natural Integration. This final stage is reached after a period of time in which you have continued to practice the skills and use them frequently in your daily life. When you reach this stage, you are able to use the skills spontaneously, comfortably, appropriately, and naturally. You will be able, on-the-spot, to recognize, initiate, and respond to events more flexibly and effectively than you ever thought possible. No matter how aware and skilled you become, do not be disheartened when you find yourself, usually in a tired or distressed state, regressing to a less effective, well-learned past mode of communication. The difference between now and former times is that you do not have to stay "stuck"; you have tools to get moving again.

Copyright © 1989, Interpersonal Communication Programs, Inc., Littleton, CO

How to Use the COMMUNICATION SKILLS WORKBOOK

Begin With the Pre-Assessment

The WORKBOOK begins with a Pre-Assessment for helping you *choose* where to focus your learning. It ends with a Post-Assessment for helping you *recognize* changes in your awareness and communication skills after studying CONNECTING.

Choose Flexibly

Throughout the WORKBOOK you will find Outlines, Quizzes, Worksheets, Interaction Observation Forms, Guidelines, and Skill Reviews for helping you expand your awareness and increase your communication skills. Material in the WORKBOOK is organized into four major sections:

    I. Communication Maps

   II. Communication Skills

  III. Relationship Maps

  IV. Relationship Processes

The sections generally progress from exercises to expand your personal and relational awareness to activities for practicing communication skills and applying them as strategies for resolving issues.

Flexibly choose material and exercises on the basis of your Pre-Assessment needs or other interests. Complete those that you think will help you become a better communicator. You do not need to begin at the beginning to work your way through the WORKBOOK.

If you are studying CONNECTING individually with a teacher, counselor ,or therapist, or if you are participating in a class or group, the coach may also have some suggestions to guide your learning, based on your Pre-Assessment and other considerations.*

Study With Another Person

We encourage you, whether you study CONNECTING individually or in a group, to find other persons with whom you can practice the skills and share your insights and gains. These people can give you valuable feedback on what you are doing that helps you or hinders you from using the skills effectively.

---

*A **CONNECTING SKILLS INSTRUCTOR MANUAL** is also available from Interpersonal Communication Programs, Inc., for use in teaching CONNECTING in a variety of educational formats and settings.

Copyright © 1989, Interpersonal Communication Programs, Inc., Littleton, CO

Tackle Smaller Issues Before Taking on Larger Ones

We also suggest that you practice using new skills on smaller and less sensitive issues before tackling really tough issues and decisions. Instead of trying to apply the skills with every relationship and issue, be selective. First, experiment in supportive relationships and with smaller issues. Soon you will find yourself handling other situations differently as well.

Maintain a Balance

Most formal education involves learning about the "objective" world "outside" yourself — in science, mathematics, technology, and accounting, for example. Relatively little attention is directed toward learning about the more "subjective" world of experience "inside" yourself and how it impacts your personal happiness, productivity, and relationships.

Learning about yourself can have enormous payoffs by expanding your choices in life. But learning about "what makes you tick" can also stir up pain and anxiety. Some of the worksheets in this WORKBOOK encourage you to examine your experiences and consider changes you would like to incorporate. Keep a balanced perspective between positive and negatives. *Focus on your own and other's strengths* as you also attend to limitations you would like to change.

Apply Important Ground Rules

As you use the WORKBOOK to stimulate personal and relational growth, apply these ground rules:

1. If an exercise instructs you to do something that you do not want to do, do not do it! Use your own wisdom and judgment in deciding which exercises to do. Likewise, use tact in practicing and applying the concepts and skills with others.

2. As you study your exchanges with others, focus on your contribution and response to the interaction. This is the part you can learn to control and the part that will impact change in others.

3. Be clear about your expectations for change. Are you looking for 10 percent, 30 percent, 70 percent, or 100 percent change in your own or other's behavior? Be realistic and specific.

4. Get help when you need it. Anytime you feel overwhelmed by what you are learning and experiencing, seek out a competent teacher or counselor-therapist .

Copyright © 1989, Interpersonal Communication Programs, Inc., Littleton, CO

In Appreciation of Virginia Satir

Over the past thirty years, Virginia Satir vanguarded a revolution in in interpersonal relationships — she understood, lived, and taught "process."

Sherod Miller began working with Virginia in 1965 when, as co-founder of the Mental Research Institute in Palo Alto, California, she was a guest lecturer at the University of Minnesota. The other of us authors in time also came to know and work with Virginia. Her theoretical perspective — modern systems and communication theory — and her practical learning methods permeate our work.

Virginia was a keen observer of human interaction, an innovator, and a tenacious pursuer of congruence in all her interpersonal exchanges. We dedicate this WORKBOOK to our memory of her as a renowned teacher and internationally known pioneer in family education and therapy.

About the Authors

Sherod Miller, Ph.D., is President of Interpersonal Communication Programs, Inc., in Denver-Littleton Colorado.

Daniel B Wackman, Ph. D., is a Professor in the School of Journalism and Mass Communication at the University of Minnesota.

Elam W. Nunnally, Ph. D., is an Associate Professor of Social Welfare at the University of Wisconsin-Milwaukee.

Phyllis Miller, Ph. D., is President of Reading Development Resources in Denver-Littleton, Colorado.

PRE-ASSESSMENT

Before you begin expanding your communication/relationship awareness and skills by reading CONNECTING or working your way through the worksheets and other materials in this WORKBOOK, we recommend that you complete the five activities provided in this Pre-Assessment Section. The five Pre-Assessments include:

1. An Important-System (Relationship) Diagram
2. A Sample "Human Checkers" Decision Dance
3. An Audio- or Video-Tape Sample of Current Communication Skills
4. The CONNECTING Communication/Relationship Questionnaire
5. Setting Your Learning Goals

You may, of course, choose to read CONNECTING and do exercises in the WORKBOOK without completing any or all of the Pre-Assessment activities. However, investing time and energy in the Pre-Assessment will provide you with:

1. A baseline for comparing and measuring change in your awareness and skills during and after your study of the communication/relationship maps and skills taught in CONNECTING.
2. A set of skills and processes identified by you as the most relevant and profitable on which to focus your learning and development energies.
3. A context to begin exploring the dynamics of important relationships and groups (systems) in your life.

Copyright © 1989, Interpersonal Communication Programs, Inc., Littleton, CO

PRE-ASSESSMENT # 1:
AN IMPORTANT-SYSTEM (RELATIONSHIP) DIAGRAM*

Most of our living and learning happens in small social systems with groups of people who form sets of significant relationships that influence who we are, what we do, and who we become. Depending on your current life circumstance, here are four basic groups to which you may belong:

1. Family of Origin — the people with whom you grew up and call parents, brothers, sisters, etc.
2. Current Family — the group to which you presently belong through marriage, birth of children, adoption, foster care, etc.
3. Reference Group — a set of people with whom you identify — friends, associates, roommates, etc.
4. Work Group — the group of people with whom you interact on a regular basis on your job.

Instructions:

1. Choose one group (from the list above) that you think would be most useful for you to reflect upon at the present time.

   Name of Group: _____

2. Look at the blank exercise forms called "Current System" and "Desired System" on the pages following these directions. You will be using those pages to diagram relationships, however, read through all the directions below before beginning to do the diagraming.

3. Take a few moments to reflect. Try to picture mentally or recall feelings about where the people in your family, friendship, or work group "stand" in relation to each other. Think of who is closest to whom, who has more or less power, who communicates to whom most often, and how much affection or tension exists among various members. Reflect on how the group members you have chosen to diagram "fit" with each other.

   (If you chose your Family of Origin but you are not currently living with them, pick an important time in your life when you were. Use, for example, age 12 or 16. Recall events, feelings, and impressions you had at that time.)

4. Now, on the form called "Current System," begin your diagram. Use the entire page. Make a rectangle to represent each person, including yourself, in the group you have chosen.

   Locate each rectangle on the page so that it represents how you see, believe, or feel others and yourself to be in relation to each other as a group. Make your rectangles square, long and thin, or anything in between. Draw them standing up on end the tall way, lying down on edge the

---

* This assessment is an adaptation of the work of Arthur M. Bodin at the Mental Research Institute in Palo Alto, CA.

Copyright © 1989, Interpersonal Communication Programs, Inc., Littleton, CO

Pre-Assessment # 1:
An Important-System (Relationship) Diagram* (Continued)

flat way, or tilted at any slanted angle. Make them any size and in any spot on the page. Let them touch, be separate, partly overlap, completely overlap or be enclosed. Draw them all alike, some of them different, or all different. Label each rectangle with the person's name it represents when you finish.

5. Next, think specifically about how communication flows between members. When communication is two-way between a pair of members, draw a line with arrows on both ends (◄———►) between those two people. When communication is primarily one-way, draw a line with one arrow (———►) indicating the direction of the communication. (If there is a great deal of communication between two members, you may wish to add one or two additional lines to represent the quantity or frequency of communication between them.) If there is little or no communication between certain members, do not draw a line.

6. Finally, place pluses (+) and minuses (-) or a mix of pluses and minuses next to the lines of communication to indicate the positive, mixed, or negative quality of relationship between members.

7. Go to the "Desired System — Worksheet." Repeat the process of drawing rectangles for the members of the group. However, locate each rectangle so that this time it represents how you wish — if you could wave a magic wand — the group would be in relation to each other.

Optional: Follow the same instructions to diagram another important relationship system in your life. (Use your own paper.)

Copyright © 1989, Interpersonal Communication Programs, Inc., Littleton, CO

Current System — Worksheet

Desired System — Worksheet

PRE-ASSESSMENT # 2:
A SAMPLE "HUMAN CHECKERS" DECISION DANCE

Background Reading: Read the "Introduction," pages 1-8 in CONNECTING. Note the basic instructions on page 2 and the sample Decision Dances on page 6.

Instructions: Imagine yourself standing, face to face, on an enlarged checker board dancing out some kind of a decision which you are making with an intimate person in your life. Using the checkerboard below labeled "Current Dance," use arrows and numbers (similar to those used in the "Introduction") to diagram a current dance you are having with this person around a large or small issue. Begin by deciding who moves first, and then trace out each move after that until you have captured the pattern.

The decision in process: _____

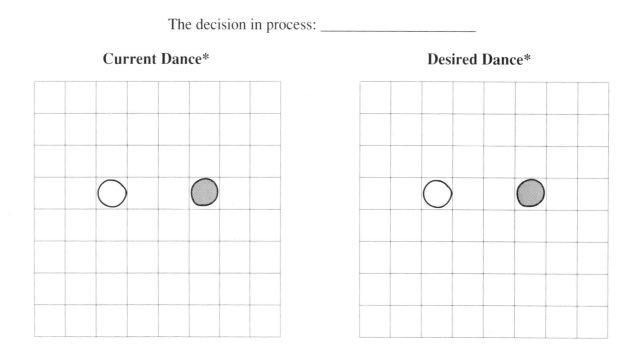

Current Dance*   **Desired Dance***

If you are satisfied with the current dance, take a moment and enjoy the pattern. If you wish the dance were different, diagram your desired dance on the board provided.

For comparative purposes, you may want to use an extra sheet of paper to diagram a second, non-intimate relationship Decision Dance.**

---

*Add more squares to the parameter of each "Checker Board" as necessary.

**Note — To start a dance, leave two squares between intimate partners, and three squares between non-intimate persons on the checker board. In intimate relationships it is possible for both persons to move onto the same square (to love or fight); in non-intimate relationships an appropriate distance (at least one square) is maintained.

Copyright © 1989, Interpersonal Communication Programs, Inc., Littleton, CO

PRE-ASSESSMENT # 3:
AN AUDIO- OR VIDEO-TAPE SAMPLE OF CURRENT
COMMUNICATION SKILLS

Instructions: To prepare for this assessment, choose someone (your partner, a friend, a family member or person at work) you think would be willing to sit with you to discuss and record the series of four *discussion tasks* listed below. When you invite the person to make the recording, show him or her the list of *discussion tasks,* and say the discussions will take about 30 minutes to complete. Each discussion is limited to five minutes.

Also explain your reasons for making the recordings. Reasons include:

1. You want to develop your interpersonal communication skills by studying CONNECTING.

2. You will use the recording to help you study your own communication patterns. (It takes considerable awareness both to participate in a discussion and simultaneously to monitor your own messages. Tape recordings are very useful for accurate feedback.) Emphasize the fact that you will be focusing on your own contribution and response, not his or hers, when you review the tape.

3. The tape will give you a before and after (studying CONNECTING) comparison of changes in your awareness and skill improvement.

Let the other person decide whether you may save or erase the tape after you finish using it.

Discussion Tasks

To make a tape recording as a part of your pre-assessment, locate:

- a cassette audio- or video-tape recorder and a 60-minute blank tape
- a quiet, comfortable, private place where the two of you can talk undisturbed
- a watch or clock to time your discussions

Even if you do not finish a particular task, limit your discussions of each task to *five minutes.* This is enough time to provide an adequate sample of your communication patterns.

Here are the four discussion tasks:

1. Plan something the two of you can actually do together.
2. Discuss in what ways the two of you are similar and in what ways you are different.
3. Pick an issue — perhaps some unfinished "business" between the two of you about which you feel some tension — and see if you can resolve it in five minutes.
4. Discuss the things that each of you does that pleases the other.

When you finish recording the *Discussion Tasks,* keep the tape in a safe place for use later in WORKBOOK exercises.

Copyright © 1989, Interpersonal Communication Programs, Inc., Littleton, CO

PRE-ASSESSMENT #4:
THE CONNECTING COMMUNICATION/
RELATIONSHIP — QUESTIONNAIRE

Here is a list of skills and processes taught in CONNECTING and this WORKBOOK. The following three steps will help you identify where to focus your skill learning for the most benefit.

Instructions:

Step 1. Mark each item twice: first with an "X" to represent your typical behavior and again with an "O" (circle) to represent your more-so or less-so desired behavior. If your typical and desired behaviors are the same, the "X" and "O" marks will be on the same number. If they are not the same, the marks will fall on different numbers.

Step 2. When you have completed marking all the items, calculate the numerical difference between typical and desired scores for each item and record the results in the "difference" column. If the "X" and "O" are on the same number, the difference = 0. If the "X" is on 5 and the "O" is on 2, the difference = 3. Note that the "O" can be located on a higher or lower number than the "X." Do not be concerned about the higher or lower direction of the scores, just calculate the numerical difference between the marks.

The numbers in parentheses under each item indicate which Chapters in CONNECTING and the WORKBOOK relate to each item. These will serve as reference guides to help you learn the skills and processes you set for yourself as learning goals later in this Pre-Assessment.

How often do you:

		Often	**Seldom**	**Difference**
1.	Recognize your impact, positively or negatively, on others? (Introduction, 1, 3, 4, 5, 14)	1 2 3 4 5 6		_____
2.	Analyze interpersonal dynamics accurately? (Introduction, 1, 2, 3, 4, 5, 6, 7, 8, 12, 13)	1 2 3 4 5 6		_____
3.	Attend to issues, misunderstandings, and breakdowns in communication? (2, 3, 4, 5, 6, 7, 9, 10, 11, 14, 15, 16)	1 2 3 4 5 6		_____
4.	Use effective styles of communication? (3, 4)	1 2 3 4 5 6		_____
5.	Identify blind spots and blockages in your awareness? (7)	1 2 3 4 5 6		_____
6.	Develop rapport and trust with others? (10)	1 2 3 4 5 6		_____
7.	Respond to interpersonal stress resourcefully? (4, 14)	1 2 3 4 5 6		_____
8.	Send clear, complete and straightforward messages? (4, 9, 11)	1 2 3 4 5 6		_____

Copyright © 1989, Interpersonal Communication Programs, Inc., Littleton, CO

	Often	Seldom	Difference

9. Attend to others' nonverbal cues as an on-going cue to your own communication effectiveness?
(Introduction, 5)   1 2 3 4 5 6   _____

10. Help others to express their concerns accurately?
(10)   1 2 3 4 5 6   _____

11. Discover the key information in a situation?
(5, 8, 10)   1 2 3 4 5 6   _____

12. Prevent or resolve impasses?
(2, 5, 11, 14, 15)   1 2 3 4 5 6   _____

13. Understand and support others' personality differences?
(6, 12)   1 2 3 4 5 6   _____

14. Turn your own and others' resistance (defensiveness) into a resource?
(11, 14)   1 2 3 4 5 6   _____

15. Make better decisions based on full, versus partial, awareness/information?
(7, 8)   1 2 3 4 5 6   _____

16. Give positive feedback (express appreciation) effectively?
(9 in WORKBOOK))   1 2 3 4 5 6   _____

17. Receive positive feedback graciously?
(9 in WORKBOOK)   1 2 3 4 5 6   _____

18. Give negative feedback skillfully and tactfully?
(11 in WORKBOOK)   1 2 3 4 5 6   _____

19. Receive negative feedback (criticism) constructively?
(10 in WORKBOOK)   1 2 3 4 5 6   _____

20. Deal effectively with others' indirect/passive anger?
(3, 14)   1 2 3 4 5 6   _____

21. Handle others' direct anger productively?
(3, 14)   1 2 3 4 5 6   _____

22. Use your own anger constructively?
(4, 9, 14)   1 2 3 4 5 6   _____

23. Track interpersonal or group process?
(Introduction, 1, 3, 4, 5, 8, 12, 13)   1 2 3 4 5 6   _____

24. Recognize and change harmful communication/ interaction patterns?
(1, 3, 4, 7, 9, 10, 11, 13, 14, 16)   1 2 3 4 5 6   _____

25. Create positive communication strategies for handling difficult situations?
(16)   1 2 3 4 5 6   _____

26. Count, rather than discount, yourself?
(5, 6, 15)   1 2 3 4 5 6   _____

27. Draw on your self-awareness?
(4, 5, 6, 7, 8, 9, 11, 12, 13, 14)   1 2 3 4 5 6   _____

28. Get others to listen to you?
(1, 2, 3, 4, 7, 9, 10, 11, 14)   1 2 3 4 5 6   _____

Copyright © 1989, Interpersonal Communication Programs, Inc., Littleton, CO

	Often	Seldom	Difference
29. Count, rather than discount, others? (6, 15)	1 2 3	4 5 6	_____
30. Understand others accurately? (6, 7, 10, 12, 13, 14)	1 2 3	4 5 6	_____
31. Initiate and manage change effectively? (1, 2, 6, 9, 10, 11, 12, 13, 14, 15, 16)	1 2 3	4 5 6	_____
32. Resolve interpersonal conflicts and difficult matters well? (2, 4, 5, 8, 9, 10, 15)	1 2 3	4 5 6	_____
33. Attend to the right time and place for certain discussions? (11, 16)	1 2 3	4 5 6	_____
34. Recognize sources of stress? (1, 2, 6, 7, 12, 14)	1 2 3	4 5 6	_____
35. Influence without being authoritarian? (3, 4, 11)	1 2 3	4 5 6	_____
36. Exercise choices in relationships? (Introduction, 1, 2)	1 2 3	4 5 6	_____
37. Experience closeness with others? (1, 4, 9, 10, 13)	1 2 3	4 5 6	_____
38. Ask for and get changes in behavior? (11 in WORKBOOK)	1 2 3	4 5 6	_____
39. Plan and negotiate collaboratively? (2, 6, 8, 14, 15, 16)	1 2 3	4 5 6	_____
40. Mediate disputes between others efficiently? (3, 4, 6, 8, 10, 12, 13, 15, 16)	1 2 3	4 5 6	_____
41. Initiate relationships? (Introduction, 5, 6, 9, 10, 13, 16)	1 2 3	4 5 6	_____
42. Recognize and deal with emotions well? (5, 14)	1 2 3	4 5 6	_____
43. Ask for and accept help? (1, 4, 9,)	1 2 3	4 5 6	_____
44. Understand group (family, work-group, etc.) dynamics? (12, 13)	1 2 3	4 5 6	_____
45. Recognize phases of development in relationships? (13)	1 2 3	4 5 6	_____
		Total Difference Score	_____

Step 3. Look over the Questionnaire above and put a check mark next to each item number (to the left of a question) with a difference score of "3" or more. (These are the skills and processes which would be the most beneficial for you to learn and develop.)

Step 4. Sum the difference scores (for Post-Assessment Comparison).

Copyright © 1989, Interpersonal Communication Programs, Inc., Littleton, CO

PRE-ASSESSMENT #5:
SETTING YOUR LEARNING GOALS

Change grows out of setting goals and following through to achieve them. Consider these criteria for setting attainable goals. Is the goal:

Conceivable — am I clear with myself as to what I want to do?

Believable — does it fit with the things I stand for?

Achievable — will I be able to accomplish it with my present strengths?

Controllable — does it depend only on me to achieve?

Measurable — will I be able to observe changes?

Desirable — is this something I really want to do?

Instructions: From the items you checked in the Communication/Relationship Questionnaire on the previous pages (see Step 3), and considering the goal-setting criteria above, list five of the items you most want to improve. Consider these as your major learning goals.

Goals

1.

2.

3.

4.

5.

After reflecting on other parts in this Pre-Assessment, write down any relationships you would like to understand better and improve as well as other relevant objectives to achieve.

Relationships to Understand Better and Improve

1.

2.

3.

Other Relevant Objectives to Achieve

1.

2.

Copyright © 1989, Interpersonal Communication Programs, Inc., Littleton, CO

Notes

Copyright © 1988, Interpersonal Communication Programs, Inc., Littleton, CO

1

THE INTERPERSONAL DANCE:
Together and Apart

OUTLINE

The Dancers — People in Relationship
A relationship, whether brief or long-term, distant or close, symmetrical or asymmetrical, is basically people dancing with each other — coming together and moving apart, influencing and being influenced, attempting to connect and sometimes failing to connect.

THE INTERPERSONAL DANCE FRAMEWORK

There are four relationship states that are each charged with positive or negative energy:

First State: Togetherness
This includes Positive Togetherness or Negative Togetherness.

Second State: Leading/Following or Pulling/Dragging
Leading/Following is positively charged while Pulling/Dragging is negatively charged.

Third State: Directing/Complying or Pushing/Blocking
Directing/Complying is positively charged while Pushing/Blocking is negatively charged.

Transition States
These comprise the second and the third state.

Fourth State: Separateness
This includes Positive Separateness or Negative Separateness.

Copyright © 1989, Interpersonal Communication Programs, Inc., Littleton, CO

FOUR PRACTICAL USES OF THE FRAMEWORK

The framework can show you:

The Big Picture — Across Time

The Current Picture — A Cross-Section

A Collage — Areas of Your Life Together

A Specific Moving Picture — An Issue Dance

VIABLE, LIMITED, AND TROUBLED RELATIONSHIPS

Viable Relationships:
These occur when the people move comfortably, confidently, and appropriately between all states.

Limited Relationships:
These occur when the people do not use all the states or spend disproportionate amounts of time in certain states, to the regret of one or both.

Troubled Relationships:
These occur when the people spend most of their time in negatively charged states — fighting, pushing, pulling the other to change, or remaining at a cold distance.

CHANGING THE WAY YOU RELATE

You can only change or control your own behavior; you can only ask for change in the other.

ACTION, REACTION, INTERACTION

Your action becomes the stimulus to your partner's reaction, which in turn is the basis for your interaction (your response to your partner's reaction in light of your original action).

Copyright © 1989 , Interpersonal Communication Programs, Inc., Littleton, CO

RECENT EXPERIENCES IN VARIOUS RELATIONSHIP STATES
— WORKSHEET

Background Reading: "The Interpersonal Dance: Together and Apart," Chapter 1, pages 13-28 in CONNECTING.

Instructions: Look at each of the Relationship States (listed below and on the following pages), and write down the name(s) of any people and a recent experience (a specific conversation, activity, or event) which you have had with him or her which represents the state.

	Name(s)	**Situation(s)**
Positive Togetherness		
Negative Togetherness		
Leading/Following		
You Lead/Other Follows		
Other Leads/You Follow		

Copyright © 1989, Interpersonal Communication Programs, Inc., Littleton, CO

Recent Experiences in Various Relationship States
— Worksheet (Continued)

	Name(s)	Situation(s)
Pulling/Dragging		
You Pull/Other Drags		
Other Pulls/You Drag		
Directing/Complying		
You Direct/Other Complies		
Other Directs/You Comply		

Copyright © 1989, Interpersonal Communication Programs, Inc., Littleton, CO

Recent Experiences in Various Relationship States
— Worksheet (Continued)

	Name(s)	Situation(s)
Pushing/Blocking		
You Push/Other Blocks		
OtherPushes/You Block		
Positive Separateness		
Negative Separateness		

Copyright © 1989, Interpersonal Communication Programs, Inc., Littleton, CO

A SIGNIFICANT INTERPERSONAL DANCE — WORKSHEET

Background Reading: Read Chapter 1, "The Interpersonal Dance," pages 13 - 28 in CONNECTING.

Instructions: Think about a significant relationship and what percent of mental, emotional and physical energy falls into each of the various relationship states (dance steps). Let "A" represent yourself, and "B" the other person. Set a certain time period — the last two weeks, month, or two months — to consider. Time Period _____ . Fill in a figure to represent how you have experienced your relationship, percentage-wise, in each state during the time period. Finally, if you wish your relationship were different in some ways, complete the "Desired %" to show your desired relationship. Feel free to add words or phrases around the diagram, which remind you of events, issues, or situations that reflect current states.

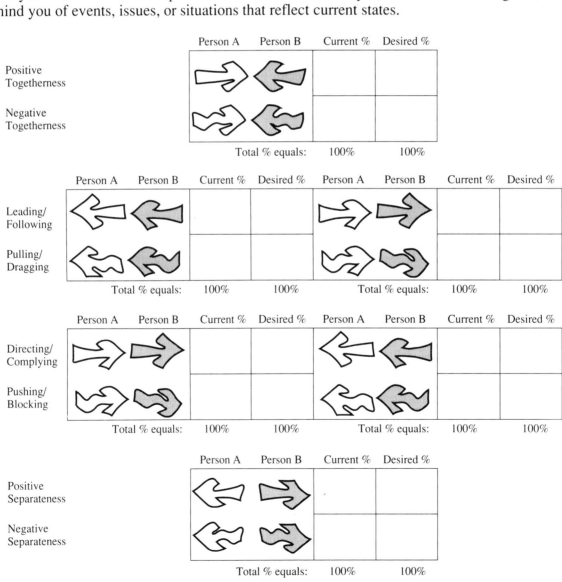

Copyright © 1989, Interpersonal Communication Programs, Inc., Littleton, CO

COMMUNICATION MAPS

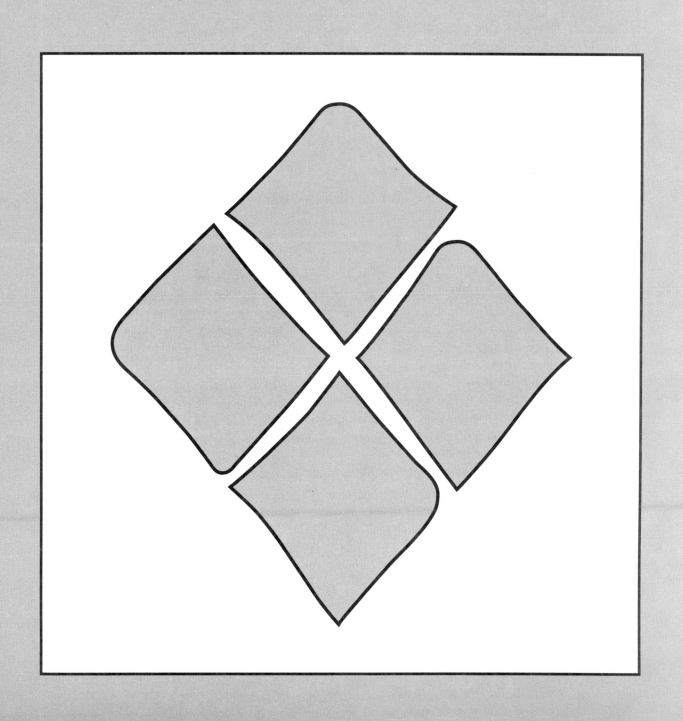

2

CONTENT, COMMUNICYCLE, AND CHANGE

OUTLINE

CONTENT: THE FOCUS OF CONVERSATION
(What You Talk About)

Types of Messages include:

Topic Messages

Personal: Other Messages

Personal: Self Messages

Relationship (You and Other) Messages

(Plus Blended-Focus Messages)

Topic, Personal, and Relationship Issues
Different issues correspond with different focuses of the messages.

Definition of an Issue:
An issue may be anything that concerns one or both parties, usually involves a decision to be made, and is important for one or both partners.

Definition of a Problem:
A problem is any issue that a person or partners are unable to resolve successfully on their own.

The Focus of Issues: Its Effect on Risk and Intimacy
The closer the issue focus is to personal and relationship areas, the more chance there is for risk and for intimacy.

Copyright © 1989, Interpersonal Communication Programs, Inc., Littleton, CO

COMMUNICYCLE: THE PROCESS OF CONVERSATION

A Communicycle is the smallest unit of a completed message and is a circular process.

The outcome of an issue is often determined by how communicycles are finished or unfinished.

Impasse in the Communicycle

An impasse occurs when one person tries to close the communicycle loop, while the other persists in focusing on another direction.

Complete and Incomplete Communicycles

A successful conversation is usually composed of complete communicycles.

Incomplete communicycles are potential turning points in communication.

THE CHANGE MAP

Issues are often the focal point of change.

Issues often arise in a "pinch message," a message which alludes to and may introduce an issue.

"Pinch messages" generate several options for dealing with an issue.

Copyright © 1989, Interpersonal Communication Programs, Inc., Littleton, CO

TYPES OF MESSAGES — QUIZ YOURSELF

Background Reading: "The Focus of Conversation," Chapter 2, pages 31 - 34, in CONNECTING.

Instructions: For each sentence below, indicate what the focus of the sentence is: (1) Topic, (2) Other, (3) Self, (4) Relationship or (5) Blended.

1. Sometimes I find it difficult to know what I really want.
2. Did you see the stunning sunset last night?
3. I feel very content when I am with you.
4. You should do that.
5. Where is Bill?
6. You seem upset. Are you?
7. I'd like to buy a new car
8. How would you feel if I treated you that way?
9. Rachel is out of town until Tuesday.
10. I feel good about the way we resolved this.
11. What's for dinner tonight?
12. Do you want to leave now, or stick around awhile?
13. I was really tired last night so I went to bed early.
14. You didn't seem interested in the game so I didn't ask you to come along.
15. What kind of work do you do?
16. I've been very restless lately.

Answers: (1) self; (2) topic; (3) relationship; (4) other; (5) topic; (6) other; (7) self-blended; (8) relationship; (9) topic; (10) relationship; (11) topic; (12) other; (13) self; (14) relationship-blended; (15) other-blended; (16) self.

Copyright © 1989, Interpersonal Communication Programs, Inc., Littleton, CO

FOCUS OF YOUR CONVERSATION — WORKSHEET

Background Reading: "The Focus of Conversation," Chapter 2, pages 31 - 34, in CONNECTING.

What you talk about — the content of your conversations — can vary from discussion to discussion. Some people talk primarily about safe topics or themselves. They seldom tune into others or talk directly about their relationship with other persons (present). Do you have a general pattern?

Instructions: First, in the square labeled "Current," estimate (in percentage) where your conversation typically focuses — Topic, Other, Self, Relationship and Blended — when you are with the person with whom you made your Pre-Assessment audio recording. (If you did not make a Pre-Assessment recording, estimate where you typically focus your conversations in day-to-day conversation.)

Current

Topic   Other

Self   Relationship

Next, choose two of your five minute "Discussion Tasks" from your Pre-Assessment audio tape, and score your comments (not the other person's) — exchange by exchange — as you play and listen to your original discussion. Place a check mark (✓) in the appropriate focus category each time the focus shifts. Use the boxes provided below.

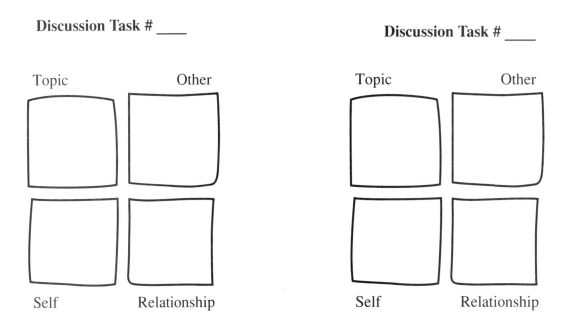

Discussion Task # ____

Topic   Other

Self   Relationship

Discussion Task # ____

Topic   Other

Self   Relationship

Copyright © 1989, Interpersonal Communication Programs, Inc., Littleton, CO

Focus of Your Conversation — Worksheet (Continued)

Over the next few days, listen to conversations around you. Notice how people manage focus. Pay attention to why you think people choose and change the focus (such as interest or disinterest, time pressure, specific purpose, discussion saturation, fear, control, etc.). Monitor your own conversations as well.

Once you are more aware of conversation focus, observe and note examples about it from one day. Percent out how you think two important people (someone in your family, a friend, an adversary, or a person at work) use focus. What do you like and dislike? If possible, experiment with focusing your conversation differently with these people or others around you. What happens? Write your comments next to the squares below.

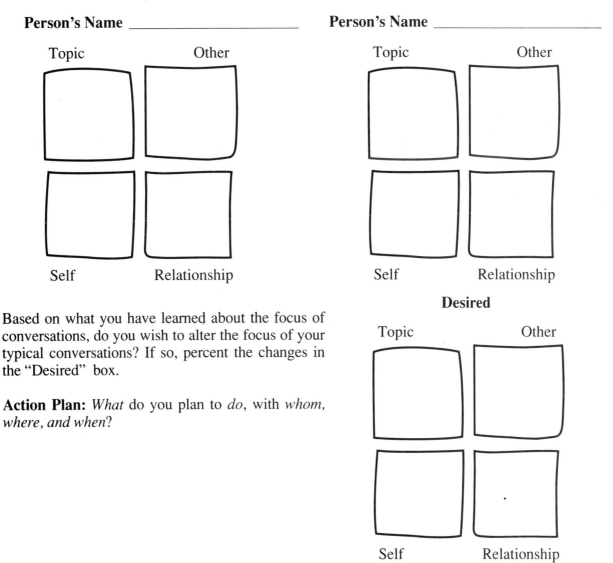

Person's Name _____   **Person's Name** _____

Topic   Other

Self   Relationship

Topic   Other

Self   Relationship

Desired

Topic   Other

Self   Relationship

Based on what you have learned about the focus of conversations, do you wish to alter the focus of your typical conversations? If so, percent the changes in the "Desired" box.

Action Plan: *What* do you plan to *do*, with *whom, where, and when*?

Copyright © 1989, Interpersonal Communication Programs, Inc., Littleton, CO

TOPICAL, PERSONAL, AND RELATIONAL ISSUES — CHECKLIST

Background Reading: "Topical, Personal, and Relationship Issues," Chapter 2, pages 34-36 in CONNECTING.

Instructions: Look over this checklist and pay attention to any specific issues which these words bring to your mind. List and specifically identify any "current" or "emerging" issues in the space provided below each list. Date _____

TOPICAL (General):

housing	food	space	chores
friends	exercise	clothes	projects
education	drugs/alcohol	transportation	leisure
work	family	sex	(other) _____
money	plans	pets	
career	time	moving/change	

Current   (briefly describe)   **Emerging   (briefly describe)**

PERSONAL (Self):

self-esteem	roles	responsibility	communication skills
identity	freedom	discipline	success/failure
energy	health	faith	attitude
values	productivity	habits	death
goals	body/appearance	creativity	(other) _____

Current   (briefly describe)   **Emerging   (briefly describe)**

Copyright © 1989, Interpersonal Communication Programs, Inc., Littleton, CO

Topical, Personal, and Relational Issues — Checklist (Continued)

RELATIONAL (You and Others)

togetherness/apartness	collaboration/competition	rules
closeness/distance	understanding/misunderstanding	acceptance
privacy/company	decision-making	boundaries
equality/subordination	celebration	conflict
stability/instability	trust	power/control
agreement/disagreement	affection	appreciation
similarity/difference	commitment	(other) _____

Current   (briefly describe)   **Emerging   (briefly describe)**

You will be asked to refer back to this Issues — Checklist as you work through the Workbook.

Copyright © 1989, Interpersonal Communication Programs, Inc., Littleton, CO

COMPLETE AND INCOMPLETE COMMUNICYCLES — WORKSHEET

Background Reading: "Communicycle: The Process of Conversation," Chapter 2, pages 38 - 42, in CONNECTING.

Instructions: Replay "Discussion Tasks" Number 1, "Plan something," and Number 3, "Pick an issue," (from your Pre-Assessment audio-tape recording). Use the space below to track and count the number of completed and incompleted communicycles in your discussions. Note any particularly influential turning points — either completed or incompleted communicycles. (If you did not make a Pre-Assessment audio tape, observe a role play or other exchange where two people are having a serious discussion.)

	Self's Completed	**Other's Completed**
Tape 1:		
Tape 3:		

	Self's Incompleted	**Other's Incompleted**
Tape 1:		

Copyright © 1989, Interpersonal Communication Programs, Inc., Littleton, CO

Complete and Incomplete Communicycles — Worksheet (Continued)

	Self's Incompleted	**Other's Incompleted**
Tape 3:		

1. What behaviors in these exchanges facilitated communicycles? What behaviors interfered with and prevented communicycles?

2. What effect did any incomplete communicycles or impasses have on the outcome and satisfaction of the discussion?

Copyright © 1989, Interpersonal Communication Programs, Inc., Littleton, CO

THE CHANGE MAP — WORKSHEET

Background Reading: "The Change Map,"* Chapter 2, pages 42-43, in CONNECTING.

Instructions: Think about yourself and another important person in your life (a friend, member of your family, a volunteer in a club or church committee, or someone in a work group to which you belong). Recall and jot down some sample "pinch messages" that you have actually said or heard. When a "pinch message" occurs, how is the signal for change typically handled? Fill in your percentage estimates for "current" and "desired" relationship or system behavior.

Sample "pinch messages":

1.

2.

3.

4.

Current ____% Planned
Desired ____% Relationship
Termination

Current ____%
Desired ____%
Renegotiation
Under Duress

Current ____%
Desired ____%
Resentful
Relationship
Termination

Share Information
and Negotiate
New Expectations

Current ____%
Desired ____%

Stability

Crunch

Choice Point

Uncertain
Return to
Status Quo

Current ____% Planned
Change
Desired ____%
Current ____%
Desired ____%

Pinch
Message

Choice Point

Unsatisfactory
Resignation
Current ____%
Desired ____%

Anger
Anxiety

Disruptive
Change

Ambiguity
Uncertainty

*Adapted and printed with permission from Sherwood and Scherer, 1975

Copyright © 1989, Interpersonal Communication Programs, Inc., Littleton, CO

3 & 4

STYLES OF COMMUNICATION:
Small and Shop Talk;
Control, Fight, and Spite Talk;
Search Talk and
Straight Talk

OUTLINE

COMMUNICATION STYLES MAP

How you talk to someone falls into categories as shown in the Communication Styles Map.

Knowing the differences among the styles and being able to use each one is central to being an effective communicator.

DIFFERENT WAYS TO TALK ABOUT THE SAME ISSUE

Style I — Small Talk and Shop Talk
Style II — Control Talk, Fight Talk, and Spite Talk

Each style has certain characteristics.

Each style has typical behaviors.

Each style has its own type of impact.

You can learn tips for handling each style.

There are similarities and differences in Control, Fight, and Spite Talk, all variations of Style II.

Copyright © 1989, Interpersonal Communication Programs, Inc., Littleton, CO

Style III — Search Talk

Style IV — Straight Talk

Each style has its own characteristics, typical behaviors, and impact. You can learn tips about using the styles.

MIXED MESSAGES

These occur when any intention or behavior from Style II slips into another style.

YOU NEED ALL THE STYLES

Each style serves a special purpose and communicates something different.

Summary Points

1. People negotiate how they are going to relate by the styles of communication they use.
2. Fight and Spite Talk try to control others by withholding information and limiting choices. Straight Talk tries to connect with others by increasing information and expanding choices.
3. Control, Fight, and Spite Talk focus on others. Straight Talk focuses on yourself, on your response, and your contribution to a situation. It demonstrates self control.
4. The style you give is generally the style you get: action, reaction, interaction.
5. The purer the style, the clearer the message. Mixed messages send unclear messages.

Copyright © 1989, Interpersonal Communication Programs, Inc., Littleton, CO

OVERVIEW OF COMMUNICATION STYLE ACTIONS

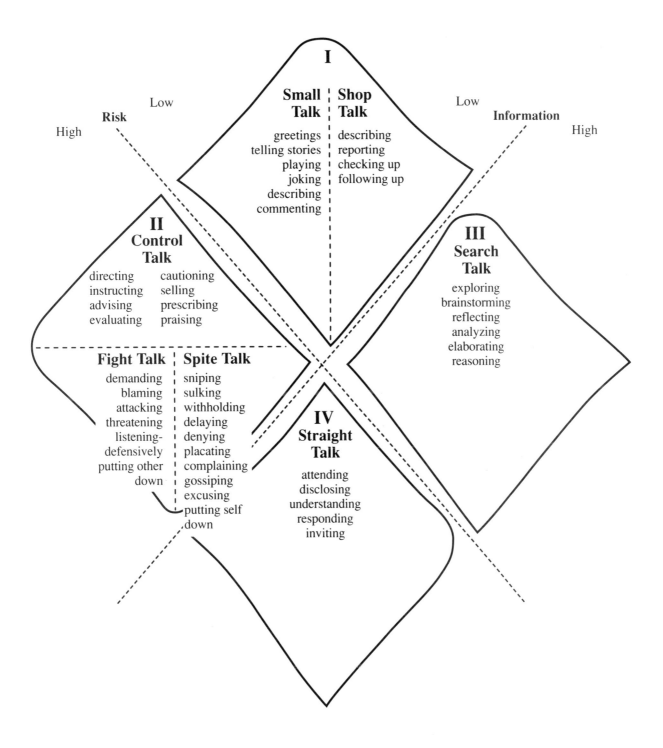

I

Small Talk

greetings
telling stories
playing
joking
describing
commenting

Shop Talk

describing
reporting
checking up
following up

Low
Risk
High

Low
Information
High

II
Control Talk

directing   cautioning
instructing   selling
advising   prescribing
evaluating   praising

III
Search Talk

exploring
brainstorming
reflecting
analyzing
elaborating
reasoning

Fight Talk

demanding
blaming
attacking
threatening
listening-
defensively
putting other
down

Spite Talk

sniping
sulking
withholding
delaying
denying
placating
complaining
gossiping
excusing
putting self
down

IV
Straight Talk

attending
disclosing
understanding
responding
inviting

Copyright © 1989, Interpersonal Communication Programs, Inc., Littleton, CO

STYLES OF COMMUNICATION — QUIZ YOURSELF

Background Reading: "Styles of Communication," Chapters 3 and 4, in CONNECTING.

Instructions: Identify the style of communication in each statement below.

Style I Small Talk   Style III Search Talk
        Shop Talk

Style II Control Talk   Style IV Straight Talk
        Fight Talk
        Spite Talk

Answers

1. After dinner, give Carla a call. _____

2. I'm avoiding the decision because I'm afraid Jack will be hurt. _____

3. What do you think might happen if we just let things ride for a while? _____

4. Did you see the game last night? _____

5. Bob just called and said he can meet with us tomorrow morning. _____

6. You dummy. If you would have just used your head a little, you wouldn't be in this mess! _____

7. Go ahead, do it your way. It won't bother me. _____

8. Tom, I want you to know how much I appreciate all the effort you put into planning and coordinating the conference. Without your enthusiasm and attention to details, it would not have been such a success. _____

9. Did you finish the math assignment? _____

10. I heard we're supposed to have a sunny weekend. _____

11. You don't care how others feel. _____

12. I'm wondering if Mark was offended when we kidded him about his shirt. _____

13. That's the last suggestion I'm going to make. No one ever seems interested in what I have to say. _____

14. Put your money in Treasury Bonds. They're the safest investment around. _____

Answers: (1) Control; (2) Straight; (3) Search; (4) Small; (5) Shop; (6) Fight; (7) Spite; (8) Straight; (9) Shop; (10) Small; (11) Fight; (12) Search; (13) Spite; (14) Control.

Copyright © 1989, Interpersonal Communication Programs, Inc., Littleton, CO

RECALL STYLES OF COMMUNICATION — WORKSHEET

Background Reading: "Styles of Communication," Chapters 3 and 4, in CONNECTING.

Instructions: In the next day or so, listen to conversations around you. Notice the styles you and others use in various situations, and the nonverbal postures and gestures associated with each style. Pay attention to how others (including yourself) respond to different style statements. After you have observed several exchanges, recall and list two messages in each style. Also note nonverbal aspects and responses given to different styles.

	Messages	Nonverbals	Responses
Style I:			
Small Talk			
Shop Talk			
Style II:			
Control Talk			
Fight Talk			
Spite Talk			
Style III:			
Search Talk			
Style IV:			
Straight Talk			

Copyright © 1989, Interpersonal Communication Programs, Inc., Littleton, CO

OBSERVATION OF STYLES — WORKSHEET

Instructions: As you observe and listen to roleplays of different styles of communication, (provided by your instructor) jot down the cues (words and body language) that signal each style. Also note any style shifts and incomplete communicycles.

Name _____

Cues: Style: Incomplete
                                                         Communicycles:

Name _____

Cues: Style: Incomplete
                                                         Communicycles:

Name _____

Cues: Style: Incomplete
                                                         Communicycles:

Copyright © 1989, Interpersonal Communication Programs, Inc., Littleton, CO

OBSERVATION OF COMMUNICYCLES — WORKSHEET

Instructions: As you watch each role play (provided by your instructor), choose one person in the exchange to observe. Jot down the verbal and nonverbal behaviors which both *prevent* and *facilitate* the completion of his or her own, as well as the other person's, communicycles.

Disruptive Behaviors:

Person # 1's	**Person # 2's**	**Person # 3's**
To other:	To other:	To other:
To self:	To self:	To self:

Facilitative Behaviors:

To other:	To other:	To other:
To self:	To self:	To self:

Copyright © 1989, Interpersonal Communication Programs, Inc., Littleton, CO

INTERACTION EVALUATION — WORKSHEET

Instructions: From your perspective, as a roleplay participant or observer, circle the evaluation number which represents your assessment of each item.

Role Play #1

		Low	High
1.	Quantity of words exchanged.	1 2 3 4 5 6
2.	Quality of information exchanged.	1 2 3 4 5 6
3.	Amount of understanding created.	1 2 3 4 5 6
4.	Degree of rapport between persons.	1 2 3 4 5 6
5.	Who controlled the discussion?	

☐ Neither
  had control
☐ Person #1
  controlled
☐ Person #2
  controlled
☐ Both shared
  control

6. Degree of trust generated between persons for future work together. 1 2 3 4 5 6
7. Effectiveness of the discussion toward resolving the issue. 1 2 3 4 5 6

Role Play #2

		Low	High
1.	Quantity of words exchanged.	1 2 3 4 5 6
2.	Quality of information exchanged.	1 2 3 4 5 6
3.	Amount of understanding created.	1 2 3 4 5 6
4.	Degree of rapport between persons.	1 2 3 4 5 6
5.	Who controlled the discussion?	

☐ Neither
  had control
☐ Person #1
  controlled
☐ Person #2
  controlled
☐ Both shared
  control

6. Degree of trust generated between persons for future work together. 1 2 3 4 5 6
7. Effectiveness of the discussion toward resolving the issue. 1 2 3 4 5 6

Feedback tip:
When you give feedback to the roleplay participants, be sure to include specific examples of the communication behaviors you observed that served as the basis of your ratings.

Copyright © 1989, Interpersonal Communication Programs, Inc., Littleton, CO

COMMUNICATION-STYLE USAGE — WORKSHEET

Instructions: Think of yourself and another significant person or group in your life in terms of the styles of communication used when you are together. What percentage of time do you individually and the other person (or group as a whole) typically spend in each style? Repeat the exercise with another person or group.

		Self		Other Person/Group _____	
		Current	Desired	Current	Desired
Style I	Small Talk				
	Shop Talk				
Style II	Control Talk				
	Fight Talk				
	Spite Talk				
Style III	Search Talk				
Style IV	Straight Talk				
		100 %	100 %	100 %	100 %

		Self		Other Person/Group _____	
		Current	Desired	Current	Desired
Style I	Small Talk				
	Shop Talk				
Style II	Control Talk				
	Fight Talk				
	Spite Talk				
Style III	Search Talk				
Style IV	Straight Talk				
		100 %	100 %	100 %	100 %

Copyright © 1989, Interpersonal Communication Programs, Inc., Littleton, CO

INSTRUCTIONS FOR OBSERVATION OF CONTENT AND STYLE
— WORKSHEET (See next page)*

Every messge has two basic parts — *content,* what is being talked about, and *style,* how it is being talked about. This exercise will help you interrelate the concepts of content and style, as well as observe patterns of interaction.

Background Reading: Chapters, 2, 3, and 4, in CONNECTING.

Instructions: Replay your Pre-Assessment audio tape of "Pick an Issue" or observe some other serious conversation. Code the interaction (each person's statements) on the matix on the next page. Assign the first person to speak a "1" in the box which represents that statement. Place a "2" in the appropriate box to represent the other person's response statement. Continue in numerical sequence. Odd numbers represent the first person's statements, while even numbers represent the second person. When more than one sentence occurs within a statement, either assign the statment to the main content and style message, or score each message change within a statement with a subscripts like, 5', 5", 5'" (indicating three messages in one statement).

Sometimes it is useful to transcribe a dialogue onto paper (either handwritten or typed) to help you track and study a dialogue. See the sample format for transcribing below.

Sample Transcript Format

Discussion Task _____

Date _____

Person #1_____   Person #2_____

What do you want to talk about?
  (Topic/Shop Talk)

                                          A tension between us. Let's see. How
                                          about borrowing money from each other?
                                             (Topic/Shop Talk)

You'll be in trouble (laughter)!
  (Other/Small Talk — joke)   . . . etc.

After you have coded your discussion, notice any patterns. What do they show? Were the content and style used appropriate for the task? When one person moved toward relationship content or Straight-Talk style, did the other person join or move away? What do you think is indicated by any large jumps across the matrix?

---

* This exercise is an adaptation of the seminal work of William F. Hill and the *Hill Interaction Matrix.*

Copyright © 1989, Interpersonal Communication Programs, Inc., Littleton, CO

OBSERVATION OF CONTENT AND STYLE — WORKSHEET

Style of Message	Topic	Other	Self	Relationship
Small Talk				
Shop Talk				
Control Talk				
Fight Talk				
Spite Talk				
Search Talk				
Straight Talk				

Copyright © 1989, Interpersonal Communication Programs, Inc., Littleton, CO

COMMUNICATION STYLES — ACTION SUMMARY

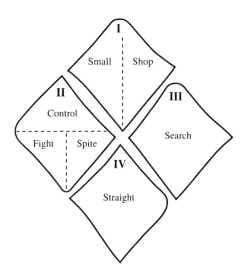

1. Which style(s) would you like to use more often?

   In what situations?

2. Which style(s) would you like to use less often?

   In what situations?

3. When used by someone else, which style is the hardest for you to respond to?

   In what situations?

(If either Fight Talk or Spite Talk is the the hardest style for you to respond to, see "Responding to Fight Talk and Spite Talk," in Chapter 14 in CONNECTING and in this WORKBOOK.)

Copyright © 1989, Interpersonal Communication Programs, Inc., Littleton, CO

5

THE AWARENESS WHEEL:
Understanding Yourself and Others

OUTLINE

THE AWARENESS WHEEL

The Awareness Wheel is a map to help you become more aware of yourself or another person at any point in time.

The Wheel includes five zones, which are distinct parts yet they interact with each other.

SENSATIONS — Your Sensory Data

Sensory data include verbal and nonverbal sensory input.

Nonverbal sources include sight, sound, touch, smell, and taste.

By looking and listening you can monitor specific nonverbals.

Reading nonverbals can give you feedback about your effectiveness with others.

Words confirm or disconfirm nonverbal data.

Intuitive sensations come from your internal world.

THOUGHTS — The Meaning You Make

Thoughts are categories for organizing meaning.

Beliefs influence your perceptions (of sensory data).

Watch for "hardening of the categories."

Interpretations represent the way you put your world together.

Expectations are how you organize your future.

Copyright © 1989, Interpersonal Communication Programs, Inc., Littleton, CO

FEELINGS — Your Emotional Responses

Feelings are your spontaneous internal physical responses to the comparison between your expectations and what you experience.

Your internal physical-emotional responses show nonverbally on the outside of you.

Instead of risky or irrational, feelings are predictable, rational, and may be positive or negative. Feelings can serve as information and are often mixed.

By becoming aware of your feelings, you can use the information to manage yourself and act successfully.

Your "rules about feelings" may interfere with your feelings.

WANTS — Your Intentions

Wants reflect core values.

Wants can be attributes you hope to be, activities you wish to accomplish, or even directions you turn to be energized.

Wants organize and motivate action and can be short or long-term.

Types of wants are: to be, to do, to have.

Wants can be for self, other, and us.

"Hidden agenda" arise from unknown or unstated wants.

ACTIONS — Your Behavior

Actions include those behaviors that are past, present, or future.

Moving from intentions to future actions means crossing the line of commitment.

As a participant and an observer, you will find it useful to become aware of your repetitive behavior patterns.

Copyright © 1989, Interpersonal Communication Programs, Inc., Littleton, CO

OBSERVATION OF NONVERBALS — WORKSHEET

What is happening "inside" is subtly reflected "outside" a person in small, unconscious, nonverbals. You can learn to recognize what change means within a person's larger patterns by observing specific nonverbals. Others' nonverbals are a major part of your interpersonal sensory data base.

Background Reading: "Sensations — Your Sensory Data," Chapter 5, pages 81-86, and Chapter 14, pages 256-57 in CONNECTING.

Instructions: Choose two people to observe over the next few days whom you are likely to see in both *calm* and *pressured* situations. In each circumstance study and later make notes (below) about the *subtle* differences you observe in:

Facial expressions	Space (distance/closeness)	Breathing
Gestures	Speech rate, pace, and rhythm	Skin color
Posture	Voice tone and loudness	Lower lip

Name _____

Calm Situations   Pressured Situations

Name _____

Calm Situations   Pressured Situations

Copyright © 1989, Interpersonal Communication Programs, Inc., Littleton, CO

JUDGE YOUR INTERACTIVE SUCCESS BY THE OTHER'S NONVERBAL RESPONSES — WORKSHEET

Background Reading: "Sensations — Your Sensory Data," Chapter 5, pages 81-86 in CONNECTING.

Instructions: The next time you try to persuade another person to change his or her thinking or behavior, take a "mental snapshot"of the other person's nonverbal state at the beginning of your discussion. Label this picture "A." As you continue the exchange, take "mental snapshots" "B," "C," etc. each time you notice a significant change in the other person's nonverbal response — toward or away from your interests. The series of mental pictures is your data base for interpreting how well or poorly you are doing as a negotiator. If you do not like what you see or hear in a "particular picture," change your behavior on the spot. For example, listen rather than talk. Does this change in your behavior elicit a different and better response? Do not keep doing something which stimulates an unwanted response.

After your exchange, use the space below to recall specific nonverbals (pictures) and your response that worked, or did not work.

Picture A   Response

Picture B   Response

Picture C   Response

Picture D   Response

Copyright © 1989, Interpersonal Communication Programs, Inc., Littleton, CO

THOUGHTS ABOUT YOURSELF — WORKSHEET

Background Reading: "Thoughts — The Meaning You Make," Chapter 5, pages 87 - 90 in CONNECTING.

Instructions: With a word or short phrase, recall and list situations in your life in which you thought you were:

In charge   Out of control

Accepted   Rejected

Valued   Taken for granted

Smart   Stupid

Attractive   Unattractive

Copyright © 1989, Interpersonal Communication Programs, Inc., Littleton, CO

THOUGHTS HAVE CONSEQUENCES — WORKSHEET

Thoughts include the *beliefs* you hold from past experience, *interpretations* and *evaluations* you make in current situations, and *expectations* you carry into the future. Your thoughts are powerful forces that shape your contribution to events.

Background Reading: "Thoughts — The Meaning You Make," Chapter 5, pages 87 - 90 in CONNECTING.

Instructions: For each of the people or groups below, list the strong *beliefs, interpretations, evaluations and expectations* (thoughts) you have about them.

Self   Partner

Family of Origin   Current Family

An Adversary   Your Work Group

Review what you have written and place a (+) next to your thoughts that *support* and a (—) next to your thoughts that *limit or discourage* change and growth in each person or group?

Copyright © 1989, Interpersonal Communication Programs, Inc., Littleton, CO

THOUGHT DISTORTIONS — QUESTIONNAIRE

Background Reading: "A Note of Caution About Beliefs," Chapter 5, page 88 in CONNECTING.

Instructions: Mark each item twice: first with an "X" to represent your *typical behavior* and again with an "O" (circle) to represent your *desired behavior*.

How often do you:

	Often	Seldom

1. Jump to conclusions on limited data?
   1 2 3 4 5 6
   Example:

2. Make assumptions that others share your perspective without checking it out?
   1 2 3 4 5 6
   Example:

3. Stereotype others — fail to distinguish individuals?
   1 2 3 4 5 6
   Example:

4. Project — assign your own thoughts, feelings, or wants to someone else, and then treat that person as if he or she possessed them?
   1 2 3 4 5 6
   Example:

5. Disregard your biases — fail to recognize that you bring to a situation experiences that color your thoughts?
   1 2 3 4 5 6
   Example:

6. Attempt to obligate with "shoulds," "oughts," and "have to's" to make others salute your opinions?
   1 2 3 4 5 6
   Example:

Copyright © 1989, Interpersonal Communication Programs, Inc., Littleton, CO

RECALLING YOUR FEELINGS — WORKSHEET

Background Reading: "Feelings — Your Emotional Responses," Chapter 5, pages 91 - 97 in CONNECTING.

Instructions: With a word or short phrase, recall and list situations in your life in which you felt:

Frustrated

Elated

Fearful

Safe

Embarrassed

Proud

Hateful

Love

Sad

Joyful

Copyright © 1989, Interpersonal Communication Programs, Inc., Littleton, CO

MAPPING YOUR FEELINGS — WORKSHEET

Watson and Tellegen's "Two-Factor Structure of Affect"* which we call the "Feeling Map" helps us understand the "rationality" and interrelationship of feelings. Emotions fall along two major dimensions — High to Low Positive Affect and High to Low Negative Affect — and two minor axes — Strong Engagement to Disengagement and Pleasantness to Unpleasantness. Each "zone" reflects a different type of energy.

Background Reading: "Feelings — Your Emotional Responses," Chapter 5, pages 91 - 97 in CONNECTING.

Instructions: Recall your feelings over the past two weeks and estimate the percent of total time you have felt the emotions described at each point on the Map. Also list the reasons — fulfilled or unfulfilled expectations (events and issues) — for your feelings.

____ %
Reason(s):

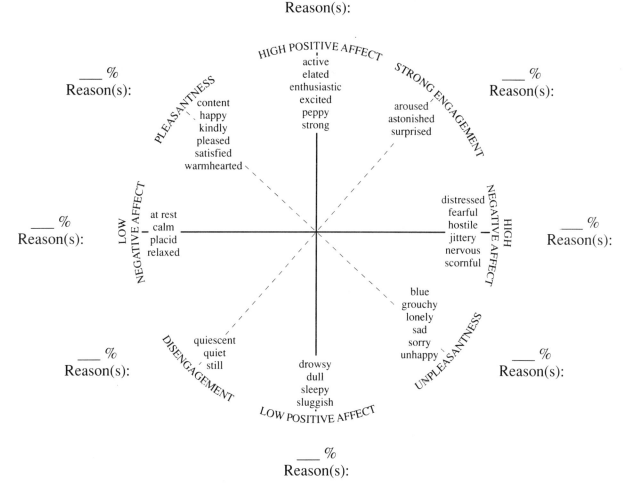

____ %
Reason(s):

____ %
Reason(s):

____ %
Reason(s):

____ %
Reason(s):

____ %
Reason(s):

____ %
Reason(s):

____ %
Reason(s):

*The diagram of "The Two-Factor Structure of Affect" is reprinted with permission of the authors, D. Watson and A. Tellegen.

Copyright © 1989, Interpersonal Communication Programs, Inc., Littleton, CO

HOW DO YOU FEEL ABOUT FEELINGS — WORKSHEET

How you *feel about particular feelings* influences what you do with those feelings — ignore, deny, hide, attend to, accept, enjoy, act on, or disclose them.

Background Reading: "How Do You Feel About Your Feelings?" Chapter 5, page 96 in CONNECTING.

Instructions: Answer the following questions:

1. List a number of feelings you enjoy feeling:

2. List feelings that you may not necessarily enjoy, but are acceptable for you to feel:

3. List any feelings that are unacceptable for you to feel:

   What do you do with these feelings?

4. List any feelings you are embarrassed to feel?

   What do you do with these feelings?

5. List any feelings you are ashamed to feel:

   What do you do with these feelings?

Copyright © 1989, Interpersonal Communication Programs, Inc., Littleton, CO

RELATIONSHIP OR GROUP CLIMATE — WORKSHEET

The "emotional climate" — range and intensity of feelings — between two people or among family, friendship, church, or work-group members can be charted on the Feeling Map.*

Background Reading: "Feelings — Your Emotional Responses," Chapter 5, pages 91 - 97 in CONNECTING.

Instructions: Choose a significant relationship or reference group and recall the "emotional climate" over the past two weeks. Estimate the percent of total time members experienced the feelings located at each point on the Map. Also list the reasons — fulfilled or unfulfilled expectations (events and issues) — for the feelings.

Relationship/group _____

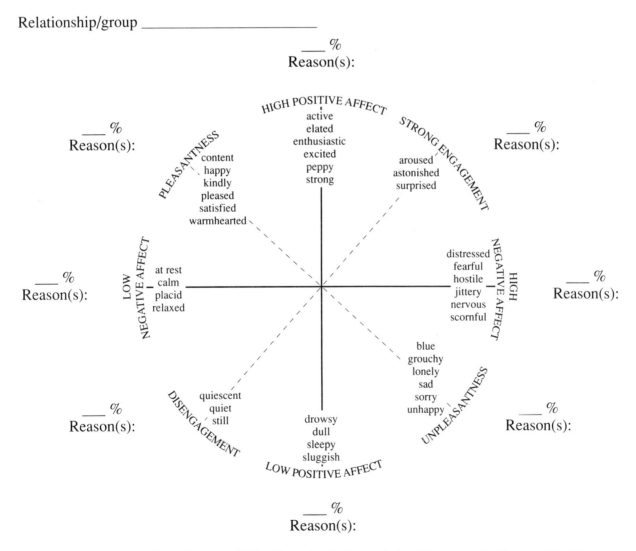

____ %
Reason(s):

____ %
Reason(s):

____ %
Reason(s):

____ %
Reason(s):

____ %
Reason(s):

____ %
Reason(s):

____ %
Reason(s):

____ %
Reason(s):

*The diagram of "The Two-Factor Structure of Affect" is reprinted with permission of the authors, D. Watson and A. Tellegen.

Copyright © 1989, Interpersonal Communication Programs, Inc., Littleton, CO

YOUR LONG-TERM WANTS — WORKSHEET

Date _____

Real wants, dreams and goals are motivators. They are the values that ultimately guide and energize your activities.

Background Reading: "Wants — Your Intentions," Chapter 5, pages 97-100 in CONNECTING.

Instructions: Use this exercise as an opportunity to reflect on what you really want in life. Thoughtfully answer the following questions:

1. What do you want *to be*:

2. What do you want *to do*:

3. What do you want *to have*:

Copyright © 1989, Interpersonal Communication Programs, Inc., Littleton, CO

YOUR SHORT-TERM WANTS — WORKSHEET

Date _____

Background Reading: "Wants are Motivators," Chapter 5, pages 98-100, in CONNECTING.

Instructions: Complete items 1 - 5 below.

1. Make a list of your short-term wants for the next two months:

2. Turn back to pages 32 and 33 and briefly review your Issues — Checklist. List any additional short-term wants that come to your mind as you review your issues:

   Issues   Wants

3. To expand your self-awareness further, go back over items 1 and 2 above and mark each of your wants according to its type: to be, to do, to have.

4. Look at your lists of long-term (see the previous page) and short-term wants. What do the lists indicate about your values?

5. Do your short-term wants move you in the direction of realizing your long-term goals?

Copyright © 1989, Interpersonal Communication Programs, Inc., Littleton, CO

ANOTHER PERSON'S WANTS — WORKSHEET

How well do you really know another person's wants? Here is an opportunity to test your accuracy.

Background Reading: "Wants — Your Intentions," Chapter 5, pages 97-100, in CONNECTING.

Instructions: Pick a significant person in your life and fill out (from that person's perspective) the following information about him or her:

Person _____ Date _____

Short-Term-Wants	**Long-Term Wants**
To be	*To be*
To do	*To do*
To have	*To have*

                                                                              Low   High
How confident are you that you accurately know the other person's wants?   1 2 3 4 5 6

At some appropriate time and place, meet with this person and show him or her this information. Confirm what is accurate and clarify what is inaccurate or unknown.

Copyright © 1989, Interpersonal Communication Programs, Inc., Littleton, CO

YOUR WANTS FOR ANOTHER PERSON — WORKSHEET

When you think of wants and another person, you are probably most naturally aware of what you want *from* another person *for yourself*, rather than what you want *for* the other person *for himself or herself*. Making this distinction between wants *from* others and wants *for* others is very important. Being aware of your positive wants for another person — based on that person's own interests with no "strings attached" — is a powerful force in connecting and building a relationship.

Background Reading: "Wants for Other," Chapter 5, pages 100-101, in CONNECTING.

Instructions: Think about an important person in your life and fill out the following information:

Person _____ Date _____

My wants *from* the other person (*for me*)

My open agenda (what I disclose)   My "hidden agenda" with "strings attached" (what I do not disclose)

My wants *for* the other person — *with no "strings attached"*

Copyright © 1989, Interpersonal Communication Programs, Inc., Littleton, CO

ACTIONS YOU HAVE TAKEN — WORKSHEET

Actions are what you *have done, are doing,* or *will do* about what you sense, think, feel, and want.

Background Reading: "Actions — Your Behavior," Chapter 5, pages 103-105 in CONNECTING.

Instructions: With a word or short phrase, recall and list situations in your life in which you:

Took initiative   Avoided responsibility

Broke a promise   Made a commitment

Sincerely prayed   Primarily worried

Played things by ear   Made a plan

Ran from something   Asked for help

Copyright © 1989, Interpersonal Communication Programs, Inc., Littleton, CO

YOUR RESPONSE TO RECENT FEELINGS AND WANTS — WORKSHEET

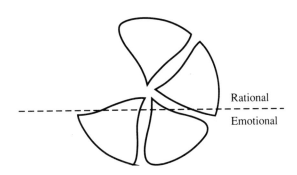

Rational

Emotional

Background Reading: "Feelings and Wants Supply 'Juice,'" Chapter 5, pages 102-103 and "Styles of Communication," Chapters 3 and 4 in CONNECTING.

Instructions: Pick three feelings and three wants (intentions) you have had during the past week. (Make sure that one of each is negative.) Now describe what you *did* (the action you took, if any) when you had this feeling or intention. Do *not* describe what caused you to have the feeling/want; rather, *focus on how you responded (behaved).*

Your Feelings

Your Action

Your Wants

Your Action

Copyright © 1989, Interpersonal Communication Programs, Inc., Littleton, CO

TAKING ACTION — WORKSHEET

Review Worksheets: "Your Long-term and Short-term Wants," on pages 60 and 61 in this WORKBOOK.

Instructions: What are you doing to achieve your wants/goals? Transfer your major long- and short-term goals to this worksheet and describe what you *have done* or *are doing* to accomplish each one. (If your goals have changed significantly since the date you originally listed them, what is the reason(s) for the change(s)? Do you have difficulty committing yourself to specific goals?)

Date _____

Long-Term Wants/Goals	**Past/Current Actions**
To be	
To do	
To have	

Short-Term Wants/Goals	**Past/Current Actions**
To be	
To do	
To have	

Copyright © 1989, Interpersonal Communication Programs, Inc., Littleton, CO

TRANSLATING WHAT YOU WANT "FOR" ANOTHER PERSON INTO ACTIONS THAT REALLY "FIT" FOR HIM OR HER — WORKSHEET

Do For Others What They Would Want Done For Themselves.

Have you ever done something special — *from your point of view* — for another person, only to have the deed go unnoticed or the gift in some way to be rejected? If so, you probably felt disappointed or hurt. When this occurs, the difficulty is not with your intention (to do something positive for the other person), but rather with your failure to do or give something valuable to the other person — *from his or her perspective.* Knowing another person's real wants — interests desires, wishes — and acting in accord with them stimulates a genuine and energized positive response.

Too often, we do not really understand others and get trapped into doing for them what we want for ourself.

Review Worksheet: "Your Wants For Another Person — Worksheet," page 63 in this WORKBOOK.

Instructions: After reviewing what you want for this person:

1. Put a check (✔) by your wants for him or her that match what he or she really wants?

2. Select two short-term wants, and one long-term want, which you have checked, and translate them into actions you can do for the other person that he or she will really appreciate.

Short-term Wants   **Actions I will Take**

Long -term Want   **Action I will Take**

Copyright © 1989, Interpersonal Communication Programs, Inc., Littleton, CO

YOUR ACTION ORIENTATION — WORKSHEET

Some people are quick to act. Others are slow to take action. Think of quick responses as being more "active," and slow responses as being more "passive." Both orientations have their strengths and liabilities — postitive and negative behavioral aspects. *Positive active* behaviors are often viewed as being pro-active, anticipatory, or assertive. *Negative active* behaviors are usually seen as impulsive, aggressive, or thoughtless. *Positive passive* behaviors are thought of as studied, careful, or cautious while *negative passive* behaviors are seen as re-active, aloof, passively aggressive, or spiteful.

Background Reading: "Participant and Observer," in Chapter 5, page 105 in CONNECTING. Review page 39, "Style Actions," in this WORKBOOK for a sample list of actions.

Instructions: On the scale below, mark your typical action orientation with an "X." Next, if you want to change your action orientation in any direction, — more or less — mark the desired point with an "O."

	Active		Passive	
My basic action orientation to life is:	1 2	3	4 5	6

Think about your actions (communication and behavior) in different situations. Using a word or phrase, categorize your behaviors from active to passive, positive to negative.

Typical Behaviors

	Active	**Passive**
Positive		
Negative		

Action Plan: Check (✓) one behavior you will practice to increase, and one behavior you will act to extinguish.

Copyright © 1989, Interpersonal Communication Programs, Inc., Littleton, CO

WHAT'S GOING ON RIGHT NOW? — WORKSHEET

Background Reading: "The Awareness Wheel: Understanding Yourself and Others," Chapter 5, in CONNECTING.

Instructions: Pause for two minutes and "tune in" to yourself — your inner-experience, conscience, self-talk. With words or short phrases, write down whatever comes into your awareness during the two minutes:

When two minutes have passed, read over what you have written and place above each fragment of your awareness the letter that corresponds with the particular zone of the Awareness Wheel:

     S = Sensory Datum
     T = Thought
     F = Feeling
     W = Want/Intention
     A = Action

1. To what extent are the various zones of the Awareness Wheel covered in your sample "flow of consciousness?"
2. Is this your usual pattern of awareness?
3. Are any zones missing? Do they suggest typical blind spots (see Chapter 7)?

If you find it confusing or difficult to categorize your awareness, review the background reading about zones of awareness and repeat the exercise. Your recognition will improve with clarification and practice.

Copyright © 1989, Interpersonal Communication Programs, Inc., Littleton, CO

REFLECT ON YOUR DAY — WORKSHEET

Background Reading: "The Awareness Wheel: Understanding Yourself and Others," Chapter 5, in CONNECTING.

Instructions: Take a little time, relax, and recall your experiences of the day. Recall the range of events, from morning to night, that were interesting, puzzling, exciting, bothersome, or whatever. As various sensory data, thoughts, feelings, wants and actions (from related or unrelated activities) come into your mind, jot them down with a word or phrase in the appropriate zone on the Awareness Wheel below. This will help you summarize and possibly savor your day as you also become more familiar with each zone of the Awareness Wheel. Be sure to cover all zones.

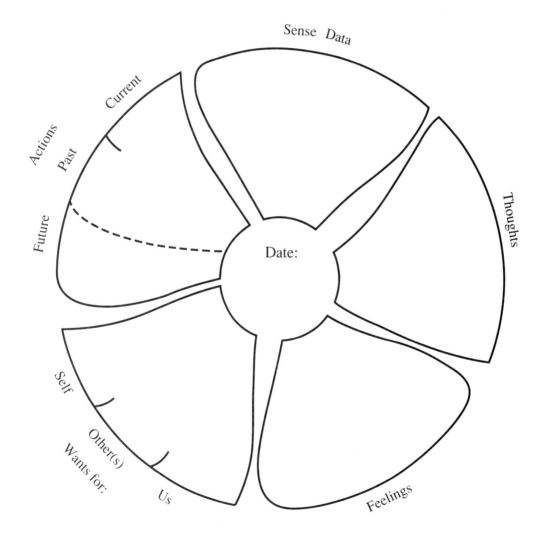

Copyright © 1989, Interpersonal Communication Programs, Inc., Littleton, CO

6

INDIVIDUAL SIMILARITIES AND DIFFERENCES:
Conflict or Collaboration

OUTLINE

PSYCHOLOGICAL TYPES

Carl Jung's theory of Psychological Types is the origin of a map of differences that correspond with the Awareness Wheel.

The map describes four complementary ways of experiencing the world.

People take in information — perceive — primarily by:

Sensing — attend most to sensory data, or

Intuiting — add seemingly unconscious associations to sensory data

People come to conclusions primarily by:

Thinking — analyze and use a logical process, or

Feeling — consider the impact on themselves or others, giving weight to what they prize

People deal with the world with emphasis on:

Openness — Perceiving — continue to become aware, live life for the process, or

Closure — Judging — want order and are outcome oriented

People are oriented to the world primarily as an:

Extrovert — turn outward to energize themselves, or

Introvert — turn inward to renew energy

Copyright © 1989, Interpersonal Communication Programs, Inc., Littleton, CO

Combining the Complements

The combinations of the complements of the four sets of differences form 16 psychological types.

The theory suggests that individuals should become aware of and fully develop their unique type.

CONCLUSIONS AND PRINCIPLES

1. There is no one best type. Each has advantages and disadvantages.
2. Similarities or differences help people connect, but also may bring conflict.
3. Similar people at first may understand one another and find a faster bonding. Later they may not receive enough synergistic energy for the relationship that differences can provide.
4. People different from one another at first may fascinate and appeal to each other. Later, the differences may put strains on the relationship. Communicating in order to collaborate is necessary.
5. In stress particularly, people revert to their most comfortable mode of operating.
6. Differences complement each other.

Learn tips for dealing with the similarities and differences in your important relationships.

Copyright © 1989, Interpersonal Communication Programs, Inc., Littleton, CO

JUNGIAN ATTRIBUTES OF COMPLEMENTARY DIFFERENCES
— GUIDELINES

Takes in information by:

Sensing	**Intuiting**
Attends acutely to five senses	Mixes associations with sensations
Sees pieces of situations	Forms general picture, impressions
Emphasizes past actions	Trusts hunches on future actions
Relives experiences	Sees possibilities, expectations
Finds details important	Resists details

Comes to conclusions by:

Thinking	**Feeling**
Analyzes and uses a logical process	Considers impact on people's feeling
Organizes facts	Gives weight to what brings harmony
Decides objectively, fairly, impersonally	Finds appeals to emotions compelling
Remains firm	Lets personal values hold sway
Lets principles hold sway	
Follows system, procedures	

Deals with the world by:

Judging (Closure)	**Perceiving (Openness)**
Is outcome oriented	Lives for experience, process
Pushes for decisions	Changes mind often, flexible
Is comfortable, after deciding, shutting out more information	Is comfortable with conflicting information
Follows a plan	Likes to let things unfold without a plan
	Is restless after a decision

Orients most heavily outwardly or inwardly:

Extrovert	**Introvert**
Draws energy from being with others and from activity	Turns inward to renew energy
Seeks others	Enjoys quiet activity
Acts with sense of hurry, urgency	Works alone very comfortably
Likes variety	Concentrates for longer periods
Wants acceptance by others	Is more reserved
Shares experiences, feelings easily	

Copyright © 1989, Interpersonal Communication Programs, Inc., Littleton, CO

A "JUNGIAN MAP" ESTIMATE OF YOURSELF — WORKSHEET

Background Reading: "Individual Similarities and Differences," Chapter 6, pages 107-115 in CONNECTING.

Instructions: From the description of Jung's psychological types in Chapter 6 and the attributes listed on the previous page, rate yourself on the scales below by placing a triangle (Δ) at the point on the scale where you believe you operate. Also briefly add an example or two to document your rating.

Take in information by:

Sensing	1	2	3	4	5	6	**Intuiting**

Examples:

Come to conclusions by:

Thinking	1	2	3	4	5	6	**Feeling**

Examples:

Deal with the world by:

Judging (closure)	1	2	3	4	5	6	**Perceiving** (openness)

Examples:

Are oriented to the outer world or to the inner world:

Extrovert	1	2	3	4	5	6	**Introvert**

Examples:

* For more instruments and readings about individual similarities and differences from the frameworks of brain dominance, behavioral styles, and psychological types, see the appendix for other materials available from ICP.

Copyright © 1989, Interpersonal Communication Programs, Inc., Littleton, CO

A "JUNGIAN MAP" ESTIMATE OF AN IMPORTANT PERSON IN YOUR LIFE — WORKSHEET

Background Reading: "Individual Similarities and Differences," Chapter 6, pages 107-115 in CONNECTING.

Instructions: Choose an important person in your life and from the description of Jung's psychological types in Chapter 6 and the previous list of attributes, estimate the psychological makeup of this person. Place a circle(O) at the point on the scale where you believe he or she operates. Also briefly add an example or two to document your rating.

Person's Name _____

Takes in information by:

| **Sensing** | 1 | 2 | 3 | 4 | 5 | 6 | **Intuiting** |

Examples:

Comes to conclusions by:

| **Thinking** | 1 | 2 | 3 | 4 | 5 | 6 | **Feeling** |

Examples:

Deals with the world by:

| **Judging** (closure) | 1 | 2 | 3 | 4 | 5 | 6 | **Perceiving** (openness) |

Examples:

Is oriented to the outer world or to the inner world:

| **Extrovert** | 1 | 2 | 3 | 4 | 5 | 6 | **Introvert** |

Examples:

Copyright © 1989, Interpersonal Communication Programs, Inc., Littleton, CO

A "JUNGIAN MAP" ESTIMATE OF YOUR RELATIONSHIP PROFILE
— WORKSHEET

Background Reading: "Individual Similarities and Differences," Chapter 6, pages 107-115 in CONNECTING.

Instructions: Copy to the scales below the rating (triangles for yourself and circles for the important person in your life) from the two preceding worksheets. Next draw one elliptical circle around your own and the other person's scores on each scale. This will give you a picture on each scale of how close or distant your psychological styles are to each other. Smaller ellipses indicate greater *similarity* while larger ellipses show greater *difference*.

For example: 1   2   3   4   5   6

Sensing	1	2	3	4	5	6	**Intuiting**
Thinking	1	2	3	4	5	6	**Feeling**
Judging (closure)	1	2	3	4	5	6	**Perceiving** (openness)
Extrovert	1	2	3	4	5	6	**Introvert**

Next use the space below to reflect on how the combination of your personal styles (psychological types) impact — blend, complement, or antagonize — each other in each of the areas listed below. First add some *positive* and *negative* implications of your profile. Then give examples of how your personal styles work *for* and *against* your relationship around each topic.

Planning/Organizing

Implications   Examples

Managing Conflict

Implications   Examples

Copyright © 1989, Interpersonal Communication Programs, Inc., Littleton, CO

Relationship Profile — Worksheet (Continued)

Recreation/Relaxation
   Implications   Examples

Handling Finances
   Implications   Examples

Trust
   Implications   Examples

Satisfaction with Relationship
   Implications   Examples

List Your Strengths
   As a Pair   Individually

Copyright © 1989, Interpersonal Communication Programs, Inc., Littleton, CO

A "JUNGIAN MAP" ESTIMATE OF A SYSTEM PROFILE

Background Reading: "Individual Similarities and Differences," Chapter 6, pages 107-115 in CONNECTING.

Instructions: Pick an important family, friendship, church, or work group to which you belong. From the description of Jung's psychological types in Chapter 6 and list of attributes on page 73 in this WORKBOOK, use the scales below to estimate the personal styles of each individual in the group. Assign each person a symbol, (for example, a square, circle, star, etc., and a triangle for yourself). Place each person on each scale at the point at which you believe he or she operates.

Name_____ ( )   Name_____ ( )   Name_____ ( )

Name_____ ( )   Name_____ ( )   Name_____ ( )

Name_____ ( )   Name_____ ( )   Name_____ ( )

Sensing	1	2	3	4	5	6	**Intuiting**
Thinking	1	2	3	4	5	6	**Feeling**
Judging (closure)	1	2	3	4	5	6	**Perceiving** (openness)
Extrovert	1	2	3	4	5	6	**Introvert**

Think about how your group is composed and functions in terms of member's personal styles (psychological types) and the following dynamics:

Harmony

Conflict

Resources

Potential Gaps (from strong similarities which may leave areas of untapped differences)

Copyright © 1989, Interpersonal Communication Programs, Inc., Littleton, CO

7

PARTIAL AWARENESS

OUTLINE

Your Mind Brings Your Experience Into Focus

Your conscious mind moves from one part of your Awareness Wheel to another.

Your Comfort Zones

People tend to perceive and understand situations from the perspective of their personality type.

Each of us has an informational comfort zone, which is the information we really trust in the Awareness Wheel.

Complete awareness means tuning into all dimensions of the Awareness Wheel in any order for a situation.

Congruence is a state of internal harmony.

PARTIAL AWARENESS

With partial awareness, some part of your or another person's Awareness Wheel is ignored, so a communicycle cannot be closed.

Three kinds of partial awareness:

Incomplete Awareness

Incomplete awareness involves blind spots (disregarding part of the Awareness Wheel), pre-closure (moving to action too fast), or being slow to reach closure.

Copyright © 1989, Interpersonal Communication Programs, Inc., Littleton, CO

Incongruent Awareness

Incongruent awareness means nonverbal messages do not match verbal messages, reflecting dissonance between parts of your Wheel.

Blocked Awareness

Blocked awareness occurs when a belief mixes with a fear of an anticipated consequence, and the result is you become immobilized. Sometimes the blockage itself, rather than a specific issue, is the real concern.

Moving Beyond Incomplete, Incongruent, or Blocked Awareness

To move beyond incomplete, incongruent, or blocked awareness may involve risk, but partial awareness usually involves personal and relationship difficulties, as well as limited options.

Learn to use the tips to expand your awareness and increase your options.

Copyright © 1989, Interpersonal Communication Programs, Inc., Littleton, CO

IN WHAT SEQUENCE DO YOU BECOME AWARE? — WORKSHEET

Background Reading: "Your Mind Brings Your Experience Into Focus," Chapter 7, pages 117-118 in CONNECTING.

Instructions: Think back to recent situations you have experienced at home, school, or work, under normal and stressful conditions. Try to recreate how your awareness unfolded in each situation. First, indicate where you entered the Wheel in each situation, and then how you moved from dimension to dimension by assigning numbers 1 through 5 — first to last — to represent your experience in each situation. If you do not recall being aware of one or two dimensions, do not include them in your diagram.

Under Normal Conditions

At home/With a partner

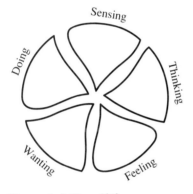

At school/On the job

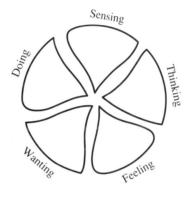

Under Stressful Conditions

At home/With a partner

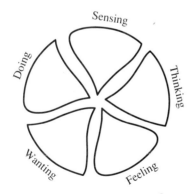

At school/On the job

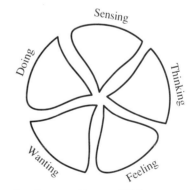

After tracking your awareness for each situation, compare the four patterns. Did you enter your Awareness Wheel in the same place each time, or in different places? Did you move around your Wheel in the same sequence, or did you have different sequences? Were you more strongly aware of one or two dimensions than the others? Did you touch each part of the Wheel in each situation, or did you leave out one or two parts? How consistent are your awareness patterns?

Copyright © 1989, Interpersonal Communication Programs, Inc., Littleton, CO

IN WHAT SEQUENCE DO OTHERS BECOME AWARE? — WORKSHEET

Background Reading: "Your Mind Brings Your Experience Into Focus," Chapter 7, pages 117-118 in CONNECTING.

Instructions: Choose two important people in your life and estimate (based on your experience with them) how you think they process their awareness under normal and stressful conditions. First, indicate where you think they entered the Wheel in each situation, and then how they moved from dimension to dimension. Assign numbers 1 through 5 to represent what you think they experience (first to last) in each condition. If you do not think they are typically aware of one or two dimensions, do not include them in the diagram.

Under Normal Conditions

Person A _____   Person B _____

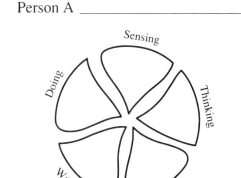   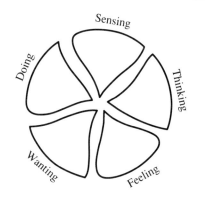

Under Stressful Conditions

Person A _____   Person B _____

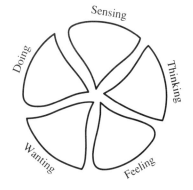   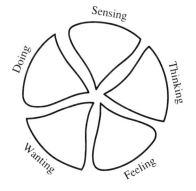

After tracking your estimate of how each person's awareness unfolds, compare your patterns with theirs. Do they enter the Awareness Wheel in the same or in different places as you do? Do they move around the Wheel in the same or different sequences? Do they touch each part of the Wheel in each situation, or do they leave out one or two parts? How consistent are their awareness patterns? (If possible, check out your estimates with each person.)

Copyright © 1989, Interpersonal Communication Programs, Inc., Littleton, CO

INFORMATIONAL COMFORT ZONES — WORKSHEET

Everyone has his or her own general "spatial comfort zone" — the range between the points at which someone is physically either too close to or too distant from another person. The breadth of this zone also varies depending on the nature of the relationship and the context in which the meeting occurs. Comfort zones of awareness operate the same way. An informational comfort zone is the information you really trust in your Awareness Wheel.

Background Reading: "Your Comfort Zones," Chapter 7, pages 118-119 in CONNECTING.

Instructions: Shade in the *three* areas of the Awareness Wheel in which you are generally most comfortable. (These are likely the zones you trust and use the most. They are the natural strengths you bring to situations.) You can call them your "informational comfort zones."

Self in general

Next, shade in both your informational comfort zones and your estimate of person A's informational comfort zones when the two of you are together in conversation. Then do the same for yourself in relation to person B.

Self   Person A _____

Self   Person B _____

Copyright © 1989, Interpersonal Communication Programs, Inc., Littleton, CO

INCOMPLETE AWARENESS: BLIND SPOTS — QUESTIONNAIRE

Informational "blind spots" occur when you repeatedly overlook, ignore, or disregard information in any zone of your Awareness Wheel.

Background Reading: "Partial Awareness" and "Incomplete Awareness," Chapter 7, pages 120-123 in CONNECTING.

Instructions: Answer the following questions to help you identify any pattern of recurring blind spots. How frequently do you:

	Seldom				Often	
1. Miss nonverbal sensory data?	1	2	3	4	5	6
2. Disregard factual data?	1	2	3	4	5	6
3. Dismiss intuitive sensations?	1	2	3	4	5	6
4. Bypass thought processes — reasoning, analysis, beliefs?	1	2	3	4	5	6
5. Overlook feelings?	1	2	3	4	5	6
6. Ignore wants for self?	1	2	3	4	5	6
7. Disattend to wants for others?	1	2	3	4	5	6
8. Pre-close — act too quickly?	1	2	3	4	5	6

From your answers above, in which zones (if any) do you most frequently experience blind spots? Are these zones outside your informational comfort zone (see the worksheet on the previous page)?

Use the space below to recall and list examples of decisions (as reflected in the questionnaire) in which you overlooked specific information which later came back to "bite" you in some way:

Decisions	**Blind Spot on Wheel**	**Specific Missing Information**

Action Plan: Identify one recurring blind spot you want to reduce or eliminate. Write down two recurring actions you will take to help you effectively attend to this area of your Awareness Wheel.

Copyright © 1989, Interpersonal Communication Programs, Inc., Littleton, CO

INCONGRUENCE: MISMATCHED PARTS — WORKSHEET

When you experience internal dissonance — pangs of conscience, anxiety, or agitation, for example — parts of your Awareness Wheel are out of alignment. You are working against yourself. Your energy is being scattered and dissipated by your internal unrest. As a result, your verbal and nonverbal actions are incongruent — forced and not genuine. Others respond with caution and even distrust to what they see and hear in you that does not fit.

Background Reading: "Incongruent Awareness" Chapter 7, pages 124-125 in CONNECTING.

Instructions: Give examples of situations or issues in which you experienced a misfit between the parts listed below. Also describe how you dealt with the dissonance in each case, for instance, ignored it, lied about it, blamed someone else, recognized and acknowledged it, changed your wants/thoughts, got more data, etc.

Examples	**How you dealt with mismatches**

Saw/heard~~~~~~~~~~~~~~~Thought/Believed

Thought~~~~~~~~~~~~~~~Felt

Wanted~~~~~~~~~~~~~~~Did

Feel~~~~~~~~~~~~~~~Did

(Other)

_____ ~~~~~~~~~~~~~~ _____

Copyright © 1989, Interpersonal Communication Programs, Inc., Littleton, CO

BLOCKED AWARENESS: BEING STUCK — QUESTIONNAIRE

Blocked awareness means you are unable to act — make a decision or resolve an issue. You are stuck. Rather than *pre-closing* on an issue, your beliefs prevent you from effectively *closing* (action) for fear of the anticipated consequences. Blockages generate anger which is normally acted out in Fight Talk and veiled in Spite Talk. Failure to act — deal with the blockage — usually results in some degree of depression — thwarted energy.

Background Reading: "Blocked Awareness," Chapter 7, pages 125-128 in CONNECTING.

Instructions: Answer the following questions to help you identify where in your Awareness Wheel you most often experience blockage. How frequently are you:

		Seldom				Often	
1. Stunned by what your see or hear?	1	2	3	4	5	6
2. Plagued by a belief?	1	2	3	4	5	6
3. Scared of the consequences?	1	2	3	4	5	6
4. Torn by conflicting desires?	1	2	3	4	5	6
5. Burned by memories of past actions?	1	2	3	4	5	6
6. Blocked from closing?	1	2	3	4	5	6

List two examples of issues or decisions in which you have been or are experiencing blockage. Draw a line in the Wheels below to represent where you were or are blocked (see page 125 in CONNECTING for sample diagram). Also describe how you did or are dealing with being stuck:

Examples   **How you are dealing with it**

Copyright © 1989, Interpersonal Communication Programs, Inc., Littleton, CO

8

MAPPING ISSUES

OUTLINE

Mapping Issues: A Process for Making Decisions, Solving Problems, and Resolving Conflicts

The process contains eight steps.

When to Map an Issue

Mapping an issue is useful when interpersonal situations are important, complicated, tension-filled, and need input for the best solution.

Map Issues by Yourself or with Others

The same tool can be applied in a number of situations.

EIGHT STEPS OF MAPPING AN ISSUE:

Step 1. Identifying and Defining the Issue
Step 2. Contracting to Work Through the Issue
Step 3. Understanding the Issue Completely
Step 4. Identifying Wants
Step 5. Generating Options
Step 6. Choosing Actions
Step 7. Testing the Action Plan
Step 8. Evaluating the Outcome

Copyright © 1989, Interpersonal Communication Programs, Inc., Littleton, CO

What Mapping Issues Does for You

The process helps you become aware of various parts of your experience (rather than having just partial awareness) to resolve issues.

ALTERNATIVE MAPPING STRATEGIES

These include situations of:
Setting Goals and Taking Action

SELF TALK

In Self-Talk, the map can be a quick guide. It can be useful when you are:
Feeling a "Pinch"
Sizing up Situations on the Spot
Handling Intense Feelings
Clearing Up Confusion
Identifying Patterns
Curbing Impulsiveness
Bolstering Confidence
Gaining Assurance When You Have to Act Fast

Realize:
Advantages of the Mapping Process
Tips Regarding the Process

Copyright © 1989, Interpersonal Communication Programs, Inc., Littleton, CO

MAPPING AN ISSUE — QUESTIONNAIRE

Instructions: Mark each item twice: first with an X for current action; next with an O for desired practice.

When you discuss an issue with one or more people, how often do you:

		Almost never					Very often
1.	Identify the issue early?	1	2	3	4	5	6
2.	Avoid the central issue to keep peace?	1	2	3	4	5	6
3.	Make sure it's the right time and place to talk ?	1	2	3	4	5	6
4.	Ask others about their objectives?	1	2	3	4	5	6
5.	Directly express your own ideas, feelings, desires?	1	2	3	4	5	6
6.	Become very persuasive for your own view point?	1	2	3	4	5	6
7.	Explore others' thoughts, feelings?	1	2	3	4	5	6
8.	Disrupt the process with irrelevant stories, jokes, or side-comments?	1	2	3	4	5	6
9.	Encourage discussion of differences/ objections?	1	2	3	4	5	6
10.	Demonstrate understanding of the other person's point of view?	1	2	3	4	5	6
11.	Withhold information for one reason or another?	1	2	3	4	5	6
12.	Suggest "just playing things by ear" as a solution?	1	2	3	4	5	6
13.	Try to superimpose your solution(s)?	1	2	3	4	5	6
14.	Seek alternative solutions?	1	2	3	4	5	6
15.	Make commitments to take action?	1	2	3	4	5	6
16.	Follow through effectively?	1	2	3	4	5	6
17.	Evaluate the outcome?	1	2	3	4	5	6

Audio/Video-Tape Option

When you have completed this questionnaire, replay your Pre-Work audio/video-taped discussion of "Pick an Issue . . . " Then, with the taped discussion as a sample of your issue-resolving communication, complete this questionnaire again. This time use a *triangle* to represent your evaluation.

Copyright © 1989, Interpersonal Communication Programs, Inc., Littleton, CO

MAPPING-AN-ISSUE PROCESS — WORKSHEETS

You can map an issue individually, with another person, or a group.

Background Reading: "Mapping Issues: A Process for Making Decisions, Solving Problems, and Resolving Conflicts," Chapter 8 pages 129- 137, in CONNECTING.

Instructions: Complete Steps 1-8 which begin on this page and continue on the following pages.

STEP 1. IDENTIFY AND DEFINE THE ISSUE

Issues can be identified by:

- Attending to your own *internal cues*— your own sense data, thoughts, feelings, wants, and actions.
- Attending to *external cues* — what you see and hear from others, events, etc.
- Generating a list of issues with another person or in a group.
- Developing individually a list of issues in private reflection.

Options for Mapping an Issue:

Individually

> If you are doing this process individually, proceed to the next page and complete the "Inventory of Current Issues."

With Another Person

> If you are doing this process with another person, and already have a specific issue you wish to map together, proceed to Step 2. If you do not already have an issue to map, each of you may independently complete the "Inventory of Current Issues" on the next page. (We are assuming that each person has his or her own WORKBOOK. If not, one person can use plain paper for writing.) After each person completes his or her "Inventory of Current Issues," share and compare issues with each other. Be sure to define and clarify any unclear issues.

With a Group

> If you are doing this process with a group, brainstorm a list of the group's current issues, and list them on newsprint or a blackboard as they are offered. Do not discourage or censor what any person brings up as an issue. The purpose of this step is to get a picture of the group's current concerns.

Copyright © 1989, Interpersonal Communication Programs, Inc., Littleton, CO

Inventory of Current Issues

Date _____

Take five minutes, relax, and think about what is going on in your life at the present time. Think of your activities at home, school, on the job, and elsewhere. As you reflect, write down a word or phrase that represents each issue that comes to your mind. If something is too personal you may choose not to write it down, but do not censor what comes into your mind. This is an opportunity to step back and see what's important to you at this point in time. (You may wish to review your "Issues Checklist" on pages 32 and 33 of this WORKBOOK.)

List Of Current Issues

_____   _____

_____   _____

_____   _____

_____   _____

_____   _____

_____   _____

_____   _____

Be sure to define and clarify any unclear issues.

Consider these five suggestions.

1. Refine issues by combining or condensing fragments of issues into larger or smaller issues.
2. If you are working with another person or group, be sure you and the other(s) understand the meaning of specific words or phrases and possess a "common language."
3. Determine the nature of an issue. Is it:
   (a) topical or a task;   (b) a personal concern;   (c) a relationship matter?
4. Decide who are the "stake holders" — persons most involved and likely to be affected.
5. Decide who owns the issue. Is the issue:
   (a) mine;   (b) other(s);   (c) ours?

Copyright © 1989, Interpersonal Communication Programs, Inc., Littleton, CO

STEP 2. CONTRACT TO WORK THROUGH THE ISSUE (Set Procedures)

Here are the major elements to consider and align as you establish your informal working contract:

- *What* is the issue we choose to discuss?
- *Who* should be included in the discussion?
- *Where* should we meet?
- *When* should we meet?

Options for Mapping an Issue:

Individually

If you are doing this process by yourself, and think this is a good time and place for you to work through an issue, choose an issue you wish to map, and write it in the hub of the Wheel (below). If this is not a good time and place for you, schedule one.

With Another Person

If you are doing this process with another person, select an issue which you have in common with the other person from your "Inventories of Current Issues." Write it in the hub of each of your Wheels (see the graphic in Step 3) and move to Step 3.

With a Group

If you are following this process with a group, set the priority of each issue and decide upon one of these two options:

1. Work on an issue now by choosing one that is appropriate for the time, place, people present, etc. If you choose this option, proceed to Step 3, by drawing a large partial Awareness Wheel (see the graphic in Step 3) and writing the issue in the hub.

2. Select an issue and schedule an appropriate time and place to pursue it. Often identifying issues, prioritizing them, and choosing which issues to map at another time and place is enough for one group meeting. Start with Step 3 at your next meeting.

Copyright © 1989, Interpersonal Communication Programs, Inc., Littleton, CO

STEP 3. UNDERSTAND THE ISSUE COMPLETELY

Fill in the partial Awareness Wheel below with words and short phrases which represent your awareness (experience) of the issue.

Options for Mapping an Issue:

Individually

After filling out your partial Wheel, reflect on what you have written; then proceed to Step 4.

With Another Person

After each person has filled out his or her partial Wheel, share and discuss with each other what you have written. (Each of you will be describing your experience of the same issue from your own perspective.) When you are finished, move to Step 4.

With a Group

All members fill out their own partial Wheel privately. Then they share and discuss their

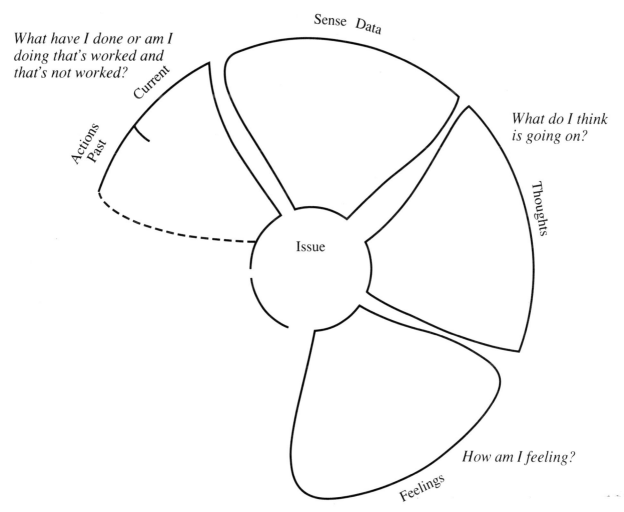

Copyright © 1989, Interpersonal Communication Programs, Inc., Littleton, CO

awareness — one dimension of the Wheel at a time — as the group works its way through the issue. As an alternative, you may want to draw a large partial Wheel (on newsprint) and have members discuss each dimension without first completing a Wheel privately. (This provides a quick and effective way to structure and focus a discussion in a meeting.) In either case, record comments on a large group Wheel or large sheets of newsprint representing each dimension of the Wheel. When you are finished with Step 3, proceed to Step 4.

STEP 4. IDENTIFY WANTS

Options for Mapping an Issue:

Individually

After filling out your partial wants, reflect on what you have written; then proceed to Step 5.

With Another Person

After each person has filled out his or her wants, share and discuss them with each other. When you finish, move to Step 5.

With a Group

All members fill out their wants privately and then share and discuss them. When you finish, proceed to Step 5.

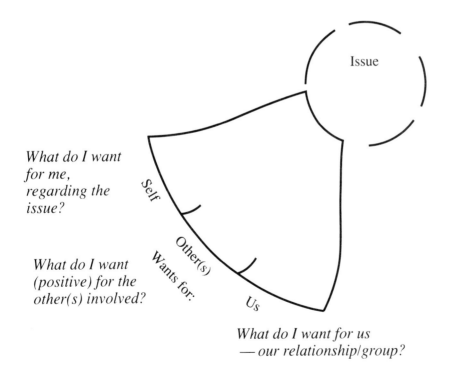

What do I want for me, regarding the issue?

What do I want (positive) for the other(s) involved?

What do I want for us — our relationship/group?

Copyright © 1989, Interpersonal Communication Programs, Inc., Littleton, CO

STEP 5. GENERATE OPTIONS

Options for Mapping an Issue:

Individually

Based on all the information you have written, generate a list of actions which you would be willing to take to resolve the issue. Then move on to Step 6.

With Another Person

Based on all the information you have written and discussed, brainstorm together a list of actions that you each would be willing to take to resolve the issue. Write them down. Then proceed to Step 6.

With a Group

Based on all the information you have written and discussed, brainstorm together a list of actions that you would be willing to take to resolve the issue. Write them down. Then proceed to Step 6.

What can I do about the issue:
- *for me?*
- *for other(s)?*
- *for us?*

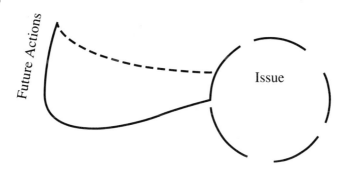

STEP 6. CHOOSE ACTION(S)

Options for Mapping an Issue:

Individually

Commit yourself to take action by choosing one or two things you will actually do. Record them as your "Action Steps."

With Another Person or With a Group

Decide which action(s) you will take and who will commit themselves to doing what. Record your "Action Steps."

Copyright © 1989, Interpersonal Communication Programs, Inc., Littleton, CO

Action Steps

```
        What I Will Do          By When

    _____

    _____

    _____
```

STEP 7. TEST THE ACTION

Options for Mapping an Issue:

Individually

After you have chosen your action step(s), test it. Pause for a moment, and visualize yourself actually carrying out each action at a specific time and place. If you experience yourself actually following through with each action effectively, great! Your future action(s) "fits." If however, you find yourself unable to take the next step, consider what is blocking you. Is it something you think (believe about the issue), feel, or really do not want to that interferes with taking action? The information in the zone(s) on the Awareness Wheel in which you find yourself "stuck" is now the central issue — the issue(s) that is blocking you. To move past the blockage, place the thought, feeling, or want (whatever is blocking you) in the center of a new Awareness Wheel, and work through (map) the blockage.

With Another Person or Group

If you are working with another person or a group, visualize your future action as described above (see working "Individually."). Share with each other how the future action fits and watch nonverbals for confirmation. If anyone is experiencing reservations about a future action, explore the hesitation. Be careful not to squelch an incongruence or blockage. This information will come back to bite you. It is more useful to incorporate the hesitation into revised action steps and gain a congruent fit (consensus) for everyone.

STEP 8. EVALUATE THE OUTCOME

Individually; With Another Person; With a Group

After you complete your action steps, evaluate them. If the outcome is pleasing, celebrate. If it is not satisfactory, re-map the issue. In any event, do not repeat actions that do not work. (See "Post Talk," page 214 in CONNECTING.)

Copyright © 1989, Interpersonal Communication Programs, Inc., Littleton, CO

SELF TALK: ANALYZING A SITUATION — WORKSHEET

Occasionally it is useful to huddle and talk with yourself about what you are experiencing and what you are going to do about it.

Background Reading: "Self Talk," Chapter 8, pages 138-143 in CONNECTING.

Instructions: Use the Awareness Wheel below to quickly think through what to do about a "pinch" you are feeling:

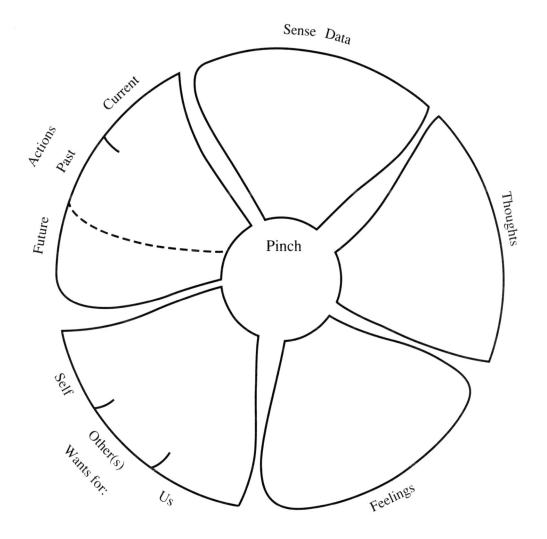

Copyright © 1989, Interpersonal Communication Programs, Inc., Littleton, CO

SELF-TALK — QUESTIONNAIRE

The Awareness Wheel is not only a very useful mental tool for understanding and analyzing issues and situations, but it is also a helpful guide for Self Talk — huddling with yourself to make internal changes which will unblock your mental, emotional, and behavioral energy.

This questionnaire has two purposes: (1) to *assess* your current use of Self-Talk strategies and (2) to *alert* you to ways you can use your Awareness Wheel and Self Talk to dissolve internal impasses.

Background Reading: "Self Talk," Chapter 8, pages 138-144 and "Blocked Awareness," Chapter 7, pages 125-127 in CONNECTING.

Instructions: Place an "X" on the number which represents how often you currently use a Self-Talk strategy to unblock your energy, and an "O" around the number to represent how useful you think the Self-Talk strategy might be for you to try in the future.

When you are stuck, unable to take action, how often do you use these Self Talk strategies:

	Seldom					Frequently
1. Gather more sensory data?	1	2	3	4	5	6
2. Re-program or re-frame (enlarge or change) your thinking?	1	2	3	4	5	6
3. Revise your expectations?	1	2	3	4	5	6
4. Work through your fears?	1	2	3	4	5	6
5. Reorder you priorities?	1	2	3	4	5	6
6. Expand you comfort zone?	1	2	3	4	5	6
7. Test alternative actions?	1	2	3	4	5	6
8. Let go of irrational beliefs or wants?	1	2	3	4	5	6

List one or two situations where one of these Self-Talk strategies would be helpful:

Situation   Strategy

Situation   Strategy

Copyright © 1989, Interpersonal Communication Programs, Inc., Littleton, CO

QUICK DECISIONS — WORKSHEET

Background Reading: "Assurance When you Have to Act Fast," Chapter 8, page 144 in CONNECTING.

Instructions: Off the top of your head, list three decisions you must make. Next quickly go across the page and fill in each part of the Awareness Wheel with a word or two to capture your awareness:

Issue:	Seen/ Heard	Think	Feel	Want	Action	%
1.						
2.						
3.						

What was this like for you? Go back and assign each action a percentage which represents your "level of confidence" that you will successfully carry out the action chosen. If your confidence is low and uncertainty high, what dimension(s) of the Wheel contribute to this most? Does the uncertainty represent a more basic issue or decision to be made? Check yourself for partial awareness around this decision.

Copyright © 1989, Interpersonal Communication Programs, Inc., Littleton, CO

FRAMEWORKS AND PROCESSES — PROGRESS REVIEW

Instructions: Rate yourself by placing an "X" in the blank to indicate where you think you presently are in the process of learning each of the CONNECTING frameworks, processes, and skills presented so far.

Review Dates: _____   _____

_____   _____

Applying Frameworks	Initial Awareness	Awkward Use	Conscious Use	Natural Use
The Interpersonal Dance				
Content of Conversation				
Communicycles				
The Change Map				
Styles of Communication				
The Awareness Wheel				
Facilitating Processes				
Attending to Individual Differences				
Eliminating Partial Awareness				
Mapping Issues				
Self Talk				
Documenting Thoughts with Sensory Data				

Check (✓) the frameworks and processes which you particularly want to attend to over the next two weeks.

Copyright © 1989, Interpersonal Communication Programs, Inc., Littleton, CO

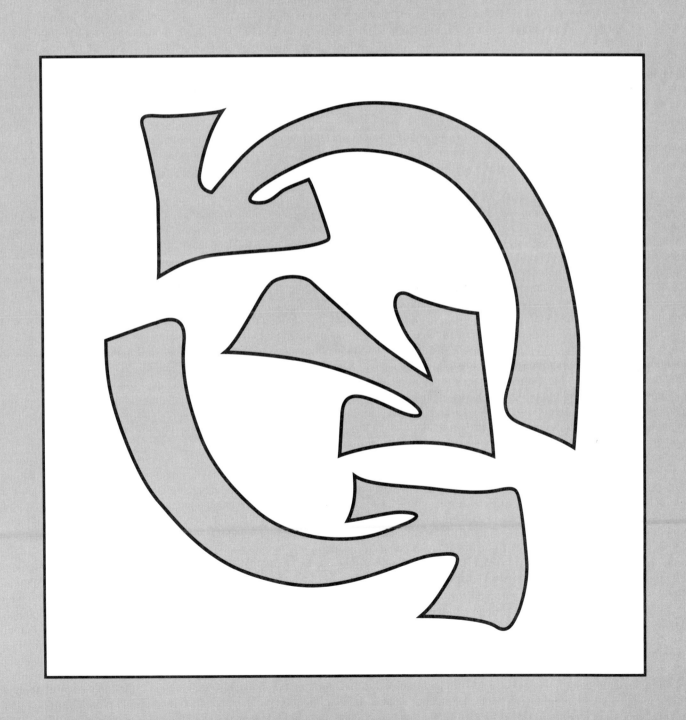

9

SPEAKING SKILLS
For Sending Clear Messages

OUTLINE

There are six speaking skills to help you state your awareness more clearly:

SKILL NO. 1 SPEAKING FOR SELF

Speaking for yourself identifies you as the source of your message.

Speaking for others produces resistance.

Over-responsible "you-statements" kindle resistance.

Under-responsible "no-one statements" lack juice.

"Poor-me statements" contain cynicism.

SKILL NO. 2 GIVING SENSORY DATA

This skill involves documenting — linking observations to interpretations.

SKILLS NO. 3. EXPRESSING THOUGHTS

This is the skill of saying what it is you are thinking, believing, assuming, or expecting.

SKILL NO. 4: REPORTING FEELINGS

With this skill you report what you are experiencing emotionally. Mostly you can report feelings without saying, "I feel."

Feelings are often expressed nonverbally.

There is a difference between *acting out* and *acting on* feelings, which involves whether or not you are aware of your feelings and whether you put them into words for appropriate use.

Copyright © 1989, Interpersonal Communication Programs, Inc., Littleton, CO

SKILL NO. 5: DISCLOSING WANTS

This skill lets others know directly what you desire to be, to do, to have.

Saying what's in it for whom can be a bonding force.

Wants are influential.

Wants stated as demands sound non-negotiable.

SKILL NO. 6: STATING ACTIONS

These statements describe what you have done, are doing, or will do.

Stating actions builds trust and confidence.

Congruence is the match between the nonverbal and the verbal, which become other people's sensory data about you.

MULTIPLE-PART STATEMENTS

These statements involve putting several of the speaking skills together.

SKILLS AND STYLES

Each of the styles draws on the various skills.

Straight Talk is the only style that integrates the affective and the cognitive aspects of communication to disclose a complete picture of the personal and interpersonal dynamics surrounding an issue or situation.

Copyright © 1989, Interpersonal Communication Programs, Inc., Littleton, CO

SPEAKING HABITS — QUESTIONNAIRE

Instructions: Mark each item twice: first with an X for current habit; next with an O for desired practice.

When you talk with someone else, how often do you:

		Almost never					Very often
1.	Get side-tracked?	1	2	3	4	5	6
2.	Express appreciation?	1	2	3	4	5	6
3.	Use an irritating tone of voice?	1	2	3	4	5	6
4.	Give specific data when providing feedback?	1	2	3	4	5	6
5.	Leave others misunderstanding you?	1	2	3	4	5	6
6.	Share directly and clearly your awareness?	1	2	3	4	5	6
7.	Talk too much and lose your listener?	1	2	3	4	5	6
8.	Credit the other for his or her accomplishments?	1	2	3	4	5	6
9.	Overtalk the other (faster, louder, or too much)?	1	2	3	4	5	6
10.	Commit yourself by saying what you will do?	1	2	3	4	5	6
11.	Send "zingers" (little put downs)?	1	2	3	4	5	6
12.	Use the other's language, metaphors?	1	2	3	4	5	6
13.	Say one thing, think, and feel another?	1	2	3	4	5	6
14.	Pay attention to your own internal cues?	1	2	3	4	5	6
15.	Tell the other what he or she should think or feel?	1	2	3	4	5	6
16.	Ask for a summary of what you have said, to ensure accuracy?	1	2	3	4	5	6
17.	Allow and use silence?	1	2	3	4	5	6
18.	Watch space (closeness/distance) between you and the other?	1	2	3	4	5	6
19.	Push for agreement before understanding?	1	2	3	4	5	6
20.	Undertalk the other (slower, softer, or too little)?	1	2	3	4	5	6

Copyright © 1989, Interpersonal Communication Programs, Inc., Littleton, CO

SPEAKING SKILLS — QUIZ YOURSELF

Background Reading: "Speaking Skills for Sending Clear Messages," Chapter 9 in CONNECTING.

Instructions: Identify the main speaking skill in each statement below.

1. Speaking for Self
2. Giving Sensory Data
3. Expressing Thoughts
4. Reporting Feelings
5. Disclosing Wants
6. Stating Actions

Answers

1. I'd like to stop now. _____

2. I get angry and frustrated when you don't follow through with what you say you will do. _____

3. You don't even care. _____

4. Wow, I'm excited to hear your voice! _____

5. I assume you are going with us tonight. _____

6. I didn't see the game last week. _____

7. I notice you're leaning back in your chair, not smiling. _____

8. I think you misunderstood her. _____

9. I'll take out the trash in a minute. _____

10. My confidence is running high. _____

11. I hope you will consider what I am saying. _____

12. I smell perfume. _____

13. I'm listening. _____

14. I heard you sigh when I called your name. _____

15. My main desire right now is to finish school. _____

Answers: (1) 5; (2) 4; (3) 3, (speaking for other); (4) 4; (5) 3; (6) 6; (7) 2; (8) 3; (9) 6; (10) 4; (11) 5; (12) 2; (13) 6; (14) 2; (15) 5.

Copyright © 1989, Interpersonal Communication Programs, Inc., Littleton, CO

SPEAKING SKILLS — EXERCISES

Fight Talk and Straight Talk

Instructions: Write out a sentence or two that illustrates and contrasts how you would tell a particular person about what she or he does that irritates you use:

Fight Talk

Straight Talk

A Complete and Concise Message

Instructions: Formulate a message, in twenty five words or less, using all six Speaking Skills, that communicates your awareness about an important matter.

Speak Another Person's Language

Instructions: Think about and develop an important message you must communicate to another person. Build the message around his or her "informational comfort zones." (See Chapter 7, page 83 on another's comfort zone, in this WORKBOOK.)

Share a Special Personal Experience

Instructions: Use Straight Talk and the Six Speaking Skills to share with an important person in your life a recent meaningful experience or insight you have had.

Copyright © 1989, Interpersonal Communication Programs, Inc., Littleton, CO

SPEAKING SKILLS — OBSERVATION WORKSHEET

Here are the six CONNECTING Speaking Skills for sending clearer messages.

1. Speaking For Self
2. Giving Sensory Data
3. Expressing Thoughts

4. Reporting Feelings
5. Disclosing Wants
6. Stating Actions

Instructions: Choose a skill to listen for as you observe two people role playing, an audio- or video-taped exchange, or a live transaction. Fill in each player's name. Then during the exchange, when you hear either player use the skill which you have chosen to observe, write down the actual phrase used. Your notes will become the basis for feedback on skill use.

First Player _____   Second Player _____

Skill _____   Skill _____

First Player _____   Second Player _____

Skill _____   Skill _____

First Player _____   Second Player _____

Skill _____   Skill _____

Copyright © 1989, Interpersonal Communication Programs, Inc., Littleton, CO

GIVING POSITIVE FEEDBACK — GUIDELINES

Positive feedback gives meaning and value to peoples' lives.

- Look for others' accomplishments — things they do well.
- Give positive feedback promptly, and only when it is sincere and genuine.
- Choose an appropriate time and place. Do not embarrass or put someone on the spot.
- Keep your message "clean." Do not use the occasion to slip in ciriticism, assign work, or ask for change.

Delivery

1. Preview your message. For example,"I have something positive I want to tell you." Knowing what to expect frees the receiver to hear and enjoy your message. Without a preview, many people expect to be criticized and do not really hear the positives because they are waiting for the "second shoe to drop."

2. Use your Awareness Wheel and Speaking Skills to enhance your feedback:

Awareness Wheel:	**Speaking Skills:**
	Speak For Self
Sensory Data	*Give Specific Data:* Describe the action or accomplishment you have observed.
Thoughts	*Express Thoughts:* Explain how this has or will help you, others, or your group.
Feelings	*Report Feelings*: Share your pleasure and appreciation.
Wants	*Disclose Wants:* Tell the person that you want him or her to know that you noticed the action and that you want the good work to continue.
Action	*Reinforce your praise nonverbally*: Shake hands or touch the person in an appropriate, supportive way.

As a way of expanding the experience, ask the receiver to describe how he or she accomplished what was done. The person's description can be a way for you and others to learn how to do something as well. Watch the receiver's energy expand as he or she elaborates on the accomplishment.

Copyright © 1989, Interpersonal Communication Programs, Inc., Littleton, CO

RECEIVING POSITIVE FEEDBACK — GUIDELINES

When positive comments are given to you:

1. Look and listen. "Drink in the moment!" Let the praise energize you.

2. Accept the positive comments by simply saying, "Thank you." And add, "I appreciate that." If you wish, say how good it feels to be complimented.

3. Do not discount yourself and your work by:

   • Dismissing it, with a comment such as, "It was nothing."

   • Disclaiming responsibility for your contribution by saying, "Everyone else (not me) really did the work."

   • Wise-cracking or making a joke out of it.

   Most importantly, do not let your response leave the person who gave you the feedback feeling foolish and regretful for having said something positive to you.

4. If others contributed to your accomplishments, give them credit as well, and when you see them, personally pass on the praise to them.

5. If asked to tell others how you accomplished something, be straightforward and take pride in telling them.

6. Look for someone else to thank or praise for something that person has done well.

Tips

1. If you have difficulty receiving sincere positive feedback, check your self-esteem — you might be a "quart low," — feeling unworthy of deserved praise.

2. When positive feedback is given effectively and received well, both the sender and the receiver leave the situation feeling good and energized.

Copyright © 1989, Interpersonal Communication Programs, Inc., Littleton, CO

POSITIVE FEEDBACK IN YOUR RELATIONSHIP NETWORK
— WORKSHEET

This exercise will help you identify how much positive feedback — credit, praise, compliments, recognition of accomplishments, thank you's, etc. — occurs in your family, friendship, and work network.

Instructions: First, write your name (on the center line) and the names of other people in your network where designated. Then before each person's name, to signify how often you *give or gave* that person positive feedback, place a + for frequently, a ✓ for occasionally, or a – for seldom/never. Finally, after each person's name, use the same symbols to indicate how often you *receive or received* positive feedback from that person.

(Give)   **Parents**   (Receive)

_____

Manager/Supervisor

Siblings   _____   **Spouse**

_____   _____   **Friends**

_____   _____

Colleagues/Peers   **You**   _____

_____   _____   _____

_____   **Children**   **Personnel in Other Departments**

_____   _____

_____   **Employees**

_____

_____

_____

4. Look at the pattern of giving and receiving. How much positive feedback occurs? Is it balanced or unbalanced? Does it go in all directions or just one or two ways? What creates these patterns? Is there any resemblence between family and work patterns? If positive feedback is low, what can you do to increase it?

Copyright © 1989, Interpersonal Communication Programs, Inc., Littleton, CO

GIVING POSITIVE FEEDBACK — WORKSHEET

See "Giving Positive Feedback Guidelines," page 109 in this WORKBOOK.

Instructions:

1. List four reasons why you, or other people, hesitate to, or do not give positive feedback:

    1.

    2.

    3.

    4.

2. Choose one person from your relationship network who has done something recently for which you would like to give him or her some positive feedback. (See "Positive Feedback in Your Relationship Network — Worksheet," on the preceding page.)

3 Fill out the five zones of the Awareness Wheel in preparation for giving the positive feedback:

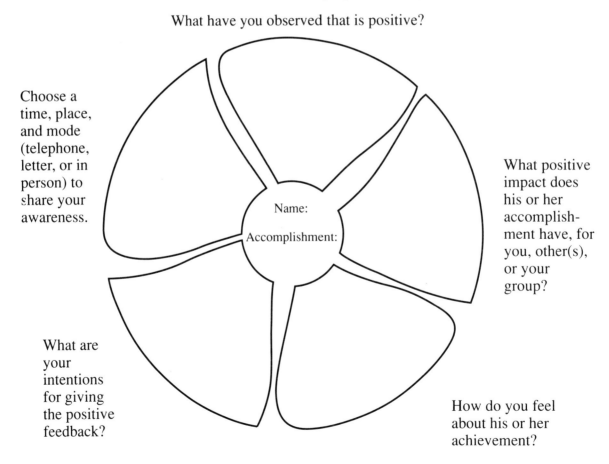

What have you observed that is positive?

Choose a time, place, and mode (telephone, letter, or in person) to share your awareness.

Name:

Accomplishment:

What positive impact does his or her accomplishment have, for you, other(s), or your group?

What are your intentions for giving the positive feedback?

How do you feel about his or her achievement?

Copyright © 1989, Interpersonal Communication Programs, Inc., Littleton, CO

POSITIVE/NEGATIVE COMMUNICATION RATIO — WORKSHEET

It has been estimated that it takes four positive "That-a-ways" to undo one negative "Gotcha."

Instructions: Choose three people you interact with frequently, and for one week at the end of each day, recall your communication with each person. Place a ✓ mark to represent each particularly positive, negative, or mixed message you recall sending each person that day.

Positive Messages = **Appreciation** — credit, praise, recognition, affection, interest, support, encouragement, thank-you's, compliments, and affirmations

Negative Messages = **Criticism** — Fight Talk,   Spite Talk, and Mixed Messages

demanding	sniping
blaming	cynical
attacking	sulking
threatening	criticizing
defensive-	denying
listening	placating
put-downs	complaining

Names:

Messages:	_____	_____	_____
Positive			
Negative			
Mixed Positive/Negative			
Missed Positive Opportunity			

Ratio = $\dfrac{\text{Positive}}{\text{Negative + Mixed}}$ _____   _____   _____

Copyright © 1989, Interpersonal Communication Programs, Inc., Littleton, CO

SPEAKING SKILLS — ACTION SUMMARY

List several key ideas from your study of the Awareness Wheel and the Speaking Skills that you want to remember and use:

List any habits from the "Speaking Habits — Questionnaire" (see page 105) that you want to change.

The six Speaking Skills presented in CONNECTING are listed below. Put a ✓ next to one or two Speaking Skills that you would like to use more often.

☐ 1. Speaking for Self

☐ 2. Giving Sensory Data

☐ 3. Expressing Thoughts

☐ 4. Reporting Feelings

☐ 5. Disclosing Wants

☐ 6. Stating Actions

Action Plan Review the criteria for setting attainable goals and the list of your five major learning goals on page 17 in the Pre-Assessment. From your pre-Assessment and the information on this worksheet, identify three specific skills you will practice or actions you will take during the next two weeks to learn new skills and change unwanted speaking habits:

1.

2.

3.

Copyright © 1989, Interpersonal Communication Programs, Inc., Littleton, CO

10

LISTENING SKILLS
For Understanding Others and Building Relationships

OUTLINE

Listening is the Key to Building Relationships

Three dynamics are involved in each relationship: rapport, control, and trust.

THREE TYPES OF LISTENING

These include Persuasive Listening, Directive Listening, and Attentive Listening.

PERSUASIVE LISTENING: WANTING TO LEAD

You listen briefly and then interrupt to disagree, give advice, or superimpose your perspective on the other person.

DIRECTIVE LISTENING: WANTING TO CLARIFY

You use questions to control the direction of the conversation.

Five Kinds of Directive Questions Include:
1. Why Questions
2. Leading Questions
3. Closed Questions
4. Multiple Questions
5. Open Questions

Directive listening has both advantages and disadvantages.

Copyright © 1989, Interpersonal Communication Programs, Inc., Littleton, CO

ATTENTIVE LISTENING: WANTING TO DISCOVER

This type of listening helps gain an overview, understand, deal with "what is," count both self and other, and connect with others.

ATTENTIVE LISTENING SKILLS (These communication skills continue on from the six speaking skills of Chapter 9.)

Skill No. 7: Looking, Listening, Matching, and Tracking

This skill involves establishing rapport — matching to create rapport — and tracking.

Look and listen for the hot spot in others' Awareness Wheels and for information "below the line" — sore spots and soft spots.

Watch the dance and watch for incongruence.

Skill No. 8: Acknowledging Messages

Join others in their zone of the Awareness Wheel.

Skill No. 9: Inviting More Information

Invite as a response.

The real payoff is getting to the core of a situation.

Skill No. 10: Checking Out/Clarifying Information

Use the Awareness Wheel and ask open questions.

Check out your interpretations.

Check out a speaker's sore and soft spots.

Skill No. 11: Summarizing — To Ensure Accuracy of Understanding

A process to guarantee understanding is called "sharing meaning," which summarizes the essence of a message.

Summarizing is useful when accuracy of understanding is important.

Either the listener or the speaker can summarize.

Summarizing shows understanding and punctuates a conversation.

Copyright © 1989, Interpersonal Communication Programs, Inc., Littleton, CO

LISTENING HABITS — QUESTIONNAIRE

Instructions: Mark each item twice: first with an X for current habit; next with an O for desired practice.

When someone is talking to you, how often do you:

	Almost Never				Very Often
1. Become distracted?	1 2 3 4 5 6
2. Listen briefly, then take over the discussion?	1 2 3 4 5 6
3. Pay careful attention to nonverbal facial and body cues?	1 2 3 4 5 6
4. Fake listening when pre-occupied?	1 2 3 4 5 6
5. Acknowledge what the other person is saying?	1 2 3 4 5 6
6. Feel or act impatiently?	1 2 3 4 5 6
7. Read between the lines?	1 2 3 4 5 6
8. Match the other's posture, breathing, energy?	1 2 3 4 5 6
9. React defensively?	1 2 3 4 5 6
10. Listen to pace, pitch, and tone?	1 2 3 4 5 6
11. "Fill in" or finish the other's message for him or her?	1 2 3 4 5 6
12. Allow the other to lead, while you follow?	1 2 3 4 5 6
13. Direct the conversation with questions?	1 2 3 4 5 6
14. Put yourself in the other's situation?	1 2 3 4 5 6
15. Inhibit the other from saying what he or she really wants to say?	1 2 3 4 5 6
16. Invite the other person to expand on his or her point?	1 2 3 4 5 6
17. Interrupt?	1 2 3 4 5 6
18. Check out the other's feelings or wants?	1 2 3 4 5 6
19. Think about what you are going to say next, rather than really listen?	1 2 3 4 5 6
20. Summarize the other's message to ensure accuracy and demonstrate understanding?	1 2 3 4 5 6

Copyright © 1989, Interpersonal Communication Programs, Inc., Littleton, CO

PERSUASIVE LISTENING BEHAVIOR — OBSERVATION WORKSHEET

Background Reading: "Listening Skills For Understanding Others and Building Relationships," Chapter 10, pages 173-76, "Persuasive Listening: Wanting To Lead," pages 176-77, and "Five Different Kinds of Directive Questions," pages 178-180, in CONNECTING.

Instructions: Listen to an audio/video tape (for example, the Pre-Assessment discussion of "Plan Something Together . . . ") or observe a role-play or TV program for Persuasive Listening Behaviors. As you observe, write down the things you see and hear — types of questions, styles of communication and nonverbal behavior — that suggest the listener is in a Persuasive Listening Mode. Also note the listener's impact on the speaker's posture, small facial muscles, breathing patterns, speech rate, pace, rhythm, voice tone, loudness, and incomplete communicycles. At the end of the exchange, rate the interaction on the Realtionship Scale.

Listener's Persuasive Listening Behaviors   **Listener's *Impact* on Speaker's Nonverbals**

Relationship Scale

	Low					High
Rapport	1	2	3	4	5	6
Control *(Listener follows Speaker)*	1	2	3	4	5	6
Trust	1	2	3	4	5	6
Resistance *(Speaker to Listener)*	1	2	3	4	5	6
Quality of Information	1	2	3	4	5	6

Copyright © 1989, Interpersonal Communication Programs, Inc., Littleton, CO

DIRECTIVE LISTENING BEHAVIOR — OBSERVATION WORKSHEET

Background Reading: "Directive Listening: Wanting To Clarify," Chapter 10, pages 177-81, in CONNECTING.

Instructions: Listen to an audio/video tape (for example, the Pre-Assessment discussion of "Plan Something Together . . . ") or observe a role-play or TV program for Directive Listening Behaviors. As you observe the listener directing the exchange with questions, write down each open question in its zone on the Wheel below. Also notice the listener's impact on the speaker's nonverbal responses — e.g., skin color, breathing, etc. Finally, complete the Relationship Scale.

Open Questions elicit descriptive information by asking: Who? What? Where? When? How? (not Why?)

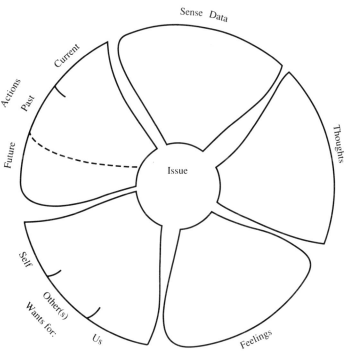

Listener's *Impact* on Speaker   **Relationship Scale**

	Low					High
Rapport	1	2	3	4	5	6
Control *(Listener follows Speaker)*	1	2	3	4	5	6
Trust	1	2	3	4	5	6
Resistance *(Speaker to Listener)*	1	2	3	4	5	6
Quality of Information	1	2	3	4	5	6

Copyright © 1989, Interpersonal Communication Programs, Inc., Littleton, CO

LOOKING, LISTENING, MATCHING, TRACKING — GUIDELINES

Look and Listen: *To Establish Your Sensory Data Base*

- Freeze-frame sight and sound of small nonverbals — before, during, and at the end of exchanges. These sensory data are the basis for your judging how an exchange is progressing.
- Watch for small visible changes in nonverbal responses — posture, minute facial muscle changes, breathing, tone, etc. These unconscious changes reflect what's happening inside. They are steps in the interpersonal dance— forward, backward, sideway, etc.
- Notice congruence or incongruence between the verbal and nonverbal.

Match Speaker: *To Gain Rapport*

- Synchronize yourself nonverbally (for example, with posture, energy level, props, etc.).
- Let the speaker lead — follow the leader.

Track: *To Register and Remember Content*

- Note complete and incomplete communicycles.
- Use Awareness Wheel to:
  Hear the story more fully by identifying kinds of statements.
  Acknowledge "hot," "sore," and "soft" spots.
  Recognize missing information.

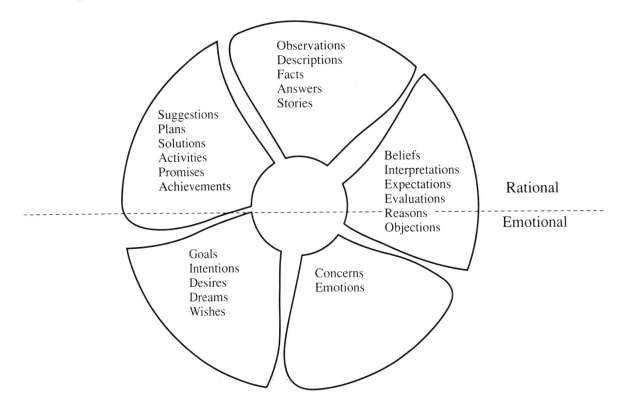

Copyright © 1989, Interpersonal Communication Programs, Inc., Littleton, CO

ATTENTIVE LISTENING BEHAVIOR — OBSERVATION WORKSHEET

Background Reading: "Attentive Listening: Wanting To Discover," Chapter 10, pages 181-202 in CONNECTING.

Instructions: Listen to an audio/video tape (for example, the Pre-Assessment discussion of "Plan Something Together . . . ") or observe a role-play or TV program for Attentive Listening Behaviors. As you observe the listener, make brief notes under each skill below about how the listener allowed (or did not allow) the speaker to tell his or her story spontaneously. Also notice the listener's impact on the speaker's nonverbal responses — for example, posture, breathing, etc. Finally, complete the Relationship Scale.

Skill #7: **Looked, Listened, Matched** (nonverbals, breathing, posture) and **Tracked:**

Skill #8 **Acknowledged Messages** (hot/sore/soft spots):

Skill #9 **Invited More Information** (one, two, three . . . times):

Skill # 10 **Checked Out/Clarified** (missing/confusing information):

Skill #11 **Summarized/Shared Meaning** (to demonstrate understanding):

Listener's *Impact* on Speaker   **Relationship Scale**

	Low				High	
Rapport	1	2	3	4	5	6
Control *(Listener follows Speaker)*	1	2	3	4	5	6
Trust	1	2	3	4	5	6
Resistance *(Speaker to Listener)*	1	2	3	4	5	6
Quality of Information	1	2	3	4	5	6

Copyright © 1989, Interpersonal Communication Programs, Inc., Littleton, CO

LISTENING TO CRITICISM CONSTRUCTIVELY — GUIDELINES

It is very difficult to receive negative feedback when you operate from low self-esteem.

While Not All Negative Feedback Fits, It Must Be Considered.

If you think someone may be displeased with you, initiate a conversation to check it out. Do not avoid criticism. Take a lot of pressure off yourself and the other person by directing the process of receiving criticism yourself.

Do not put yourself down by thinking:

- "I shouldn't have to ask; it's the other person's job to tell me if things aren't right."
- "I can't handle criticism."
- "I'm not important enough to get the straight scoop."

When You Receive Criticism, Focus on Understanding What Is Being Said by:

1. Inviting the person to be direct, specific, and complete with you in his or her criticism.
2. Asking what the specific change he or she has in mind would look like.
3. Summarizing what you have heard the other person say, to his or her satisfaction.
4. Asking if there is any other negative feedback, to be sure all criticism has been aired.

Respond to the Criticism by:

1. Acknowledging your own feelings.
2. Looking for ways to make positive use of the feedback.
3. Saying what you "buy into" and what you see differently. Share your Awareness Wheel in Straight Talk.
4. Stating your future action — what you will do to improve the situation, if helpful.
5. Making sure all criticisms, comments, and questions are at rest. Pay attention to your own internal congruence, and ask the other person if he or she has any incomplete communicycles.
6. Thank the other person for his or her courage and honesty, and sincerely ask for follow-up feedback (either positive or negative) on your efforts to change.
7. Experiment with making the changes suggested, and watch for other people's responses to your change.

Tips

1. Avoid planning a rebuttal or interrupting throughout the exchange. Stay out of Fight and Spite Talk. Stay in Search or Straight Talk.
2. Recognize that some negative feedback is a disguised request to be heard. In these circumstances, look for the bigger issue behind the criticism.
3. Feedback is subjective and not always valid. Do not let your self-worth rise and fall on one person's perspective. When in doubt, get a second opinion.

Copyright © 1989, Interpersonal Communication Programs, Inc., Littleton, CO

OBSERVE AND INFLUENCE A MEETING — EXERCISE

To increase your awareness of group process, at the next meeting you attend:

1. Notice the different styles of communication used. What styles, if any, are not used?

2. Listen for the different parts of the Awareness Wheel. Are agenda items completely mapped? What effect do missing parts have on the meeting?

3. Watch for incomplete communicycles.

At the same, or at a different meeting, experiment with these two skills:

1. *Inviting* people to say more about their ideas, concerns.

2. *Checking Out/Clarifying* missing and unclear parts of the Wheel.

After the meeting is over, assess your contribution. Did using either of these two skills create productive turning points that moved things ahead to a better understanding and outcome?

Copyright © 1989, Interpersonal Communication Programs, Inc., Littleton, CO

LISTENING SKILLS — ACTION SUMMARY

List several key ideas from your study of the Listening Skills that you want to remember and use:

List any habits from the "Listening Habits — Questionnaire" (see page 117) that you want to change.

Listed below are the five Listening Skills presented in CONNECTING. Put an X next to one or two Listening Skills which you would like to use more often.

☐   7. Looking, Listening, Matching, Tracking

☐   8. Acknowledging Messages

☐   9. Inviting More Information

☐ 10. Checking Out/Clarifying Information

☐ 11. Summarizing — To Ensure Accuracy Of Understanding

Action Plan: Review the criteria for setting attainable goals and the list of your five major learning goals on page 17 in the Pre-Assessment. From your Pre-Assessment and the information on this worksheet, identify three specific skills you will practice or actions you will take. During the next two weeks carry out the actions to learn new skills and change unwanted listening habits.

1.

2.

3.

Copyright © 1989, Interpersonal Communication Programs, Inc., Littleton, CO

11

META TALK:
Talk About Talk

OUTLINE

Meta Talk is in contrast to the Plain Talk that carries your messages.
Plain Talk involves different levels of:

Focus, Style, and Awareness
Speaking and Listening Skills

META TALK

Meta Talk is talking about the process of your interaction — the pattern or way in which you and the other person relate.

Meta Talk Skills

These skills revolve around three time elements of a conversation: Pre-Talk; Now-Talk; and Post-Talk.

PRE-TALK

This anticipates, overviews, or sets the stage for an upcoming discussion.
The skills include:
Contracting: Setting Procedures Together
Previewing (Letting the Other Person Know What to Expect from You)
Defusing and Disarming Resistance
Instructing/Coaching

Copyright © 1989, Interpersonal Communication Programs, Inc., Littleton, CO

NOW-TALK

This focuses on what is happening at the moment in the interaction.

The skills include:

Observing and Giving Feedback

Clarifying

Summarizing

Describing

POST-TALK

This is reflection on the conversation, with an eye to continuing or improving it in the future.

The skills include:

Recounting

Analyzing

Clearing the Air by Acknowledging, Apologizing, or Asking for Forgiveness

STORIES

Stories are a form of metacommunication — they are talk about life.

Copyright © 1989, Interpersonal Communication Programs, Inc., Littleton, CO

META TALK STATEMENTS — WORKSHEET

Now-Talk

Pre-Talk   Post-Talk

Background Reading: "Meta Talk," Chapter 11, pages 205-216, in CONNECTING.

Instructions: In the space below, write out several feasible Pre-, Now-, and Post-Talk Statements, which you imagine would enrich a conversation you must have soon with someone about a current issue.

Pre-Talk

Now-Talk

Post-Talk

Copyright © 1989, Interpersonal Communication Programs, Inc., Littleton, CO

RESPONDING TO MIXED MESSAGES WITH "NOW-TALK" — WORKSHEET

A Mixed message is a statement in any style, mixed with a verbal or tonal undercurrent of Style II — Control, Fight, or Spite. It usually creates distance by stimulating uncertainty, confusion, or misunderstanding. The first step in dealing with a mixed message is to *recognize* it. The second step is to *clarify* the message by commenting on it.

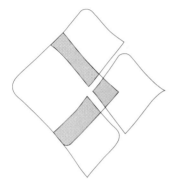

Background Reading: "Mixed Messages," Chapter 4, pages 75-77, and "Now Talk," Chapter 11, pages 212-214, in CONNECTING.

Instructions: In the space below, respond to the sample mixed messages by writing out a brief statement which demonstrates 1) your *identification* of the undercurrent in the message and 2) your ability to *clarify* the message by commenting on (unscrambling) the message. Use Now-Talk and Speaking Skills.

Mixed Messages:

Undercurrent (usually expressed in "loaded" Style II words, tone, or gestures):
   "Wish I had money to blow like that."

Presumption:
   "Since you usually don't have time, we didn't invite you."

But or yes but:
   "I agree with what you are saying, but it won't work."

Condition:
   "I'm going to stop smoking when you stop."

Build-up, put down (positive-negative):
   "You sure look nice tonight. Too bad it takes you so long to get dressed and made up."

Copyright © 1989, Interpersonal Communication Programs, Inc., Littleton, CO

THE META-CYCLE PROCESS FOR INITIATING AND REINFORCING CHANGE — DIAGRAM

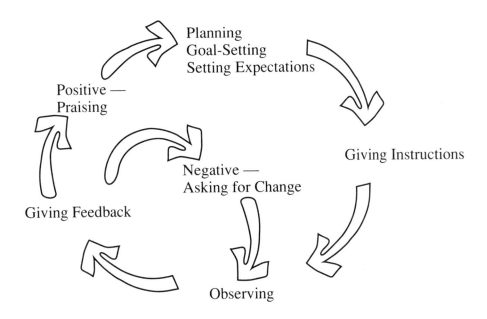

Planning
Goal-Setting
Setting Expectations

Positive —
Praising

Giving Instructions

Negative —
Asking for Change

Giving Feedback

Observing

The Meta-Cycle Process is an important map for understanding how to initiate and reinforce positive change effectively in interpersonal communication and relationships. Considerable anger, confusion, misunderstanding, and breakdown in communication result from not knowing or repeatedly overlooking or disregarding componets of the Meta-Cycle Process.

Guidelines for Components of the Meta-Cycle Process follow in this section and in other parts of the WORKBOOK as indicated below:

Planning/Setting Goals

Giving Clear Instructions

Observing (See the The Awareness Wheel, Chapter 5, pages 51 and 52, in WORKBOOK.)

Giving Negative Feedback — Asking for Change

Listening to Criticism Constructively (See Listening Skills, Chapter 10, page 122, in WORKBOOK.)

Giving Positive Feedback (See Speaking Skills, Chapter 9, page 109 in WORKBOOK.)

Receiving Positive Feedback (See Speaking Skills, Chapter 9, page 110 in WORKBOOK.)

Copyright © 1989, Interpersonal Communication Programs, Inc., Littleton, CO

PLANNING AND GOAL SETTING — GUIDELINES

When plans affect more than yourself, involve all stake holders in the goal-setting process whenever possible.

Here is a suggested strategy to follow:

Step 1.   Brainstorm *wants* (goals), including *musts* (necessities, constraints, deadlines, etc.).

Step 2.   Cluster, condense, and prioritize *wants* and *musts* into a list of challenging but attainable goals.*

Step 3.   Visualize what achieving each goal would look like in actual behavioral terms.

Step 4.   Generate a list of specific actions for achieving each goal.

Step 5.   Raise and resolve objections and anticipate obstacles.
  • For example, are there adequate incentives and benefits — for self, other(s), and us — for achieving the goals? Watch participant's nonverbals for "non-fit" cues.

Step 6.   Translate Steps 1-5 into a concise and clearly agreed upon set of goals.
  • Put each goal, and the specific action-step information, on a 3x5 card for periodic review.
  • Tag the action steps with time lines and the name of each person responsible for implementing those actions.

Step 7.   Test the goals set quickly. Ask stake holders what they *think* and *feel* about the goals set.
  • Look and listen for nonverbals which suggest incomplete communicycles and unaccounted-for resistence.

---

*See Pre-Assessment, "Setting Learning Goals — Worksheet, 'Criteria for Setting Attainable Goals,' " page 17 in the WORKBOOK.

Copyright © 1989, Interpersonal Communication Programs, Inc., Littleton, CO

GIVING CLEAR INSTRUCTIONS — GUIDELINES

Clear instructions answer these six questions:

- Who?
- What?
- Where?
- When?
- How?
- Why (provides the reason)?

Make sure the message sent is the message received:

1. The more certain you are that all six "bits" of information are accurately understood, the more confident you can be that instructions will be followed satisfactorily.

2. To determine if your instructions have been adequately understood, ask the receiver to summarize what he or she understands the instructions to be. (See "Skill No. 11: Summarizing — To ensure Accuracy of Understanding," Chapter 10, pages 195-199 in CONNECTING.) Occasionally a receiver will give you a summary spontaneously. If the summary is not accurate or is missing important information, clarify your instructions and ask for another summary.

3. As a sender, pay particular attention to the receiver's nonverbal clues that suggest he or she is not understanding or accepting your instructions. If you have any uncertainty, Now-Talk — comment on what you see and hear. Then ask for the receiver's input. Stay with the clarification process until you feel confident your communicycle is complete.

4. When a receiver is pre-occupied, even the clearest instructions may not register. The receiver is literally on a different channel. The quickest way to get the receivers to leave their channel and tune into yours is to get them to move physically — stand up, sit down, step into another area — anything that will help them "break state" and shift their attention.

Copyright © 1989, Interpersonal Communication Programs, Inc., Littleton, CO

GIVING NEGATIVE FEEDBACK AND
ASKING FOR CHANGE — GUIDELINES

Asking for change can be difficult for three reasons: (1) it carries an element of criticism and dissatisfaction with what is, which can threaten the receiver's self-esteem; (2) it implies (more or less) that "you must change" as a condition of our on-going relationship; and (3) it tends to overlook the sender's contribution/response — the interactional aspects of the situation.

Preparation

1. When you feel a "pinch" calling for change, act promptly. Don't "stuff it." Do not let the issue build to a crisis or go unattended, causing harm later.

2. Use the Awareness Wheel to organize your awareness on paper or as Self Talk in your head.

3. Think about the receiver's psychologtical type and informational comfort zones as you frame your message in order to gain the best hearing. Number the parts of your Wheel, from 1-5, in the order you think will be the most effective sequence for delivering your message.

4. Formulate any brief Pre-Talk message which will set the stage and enhance the receiver's receptiveness.

5. Visualize yourself using an appropriate style of communication and stating your message in one minute or less. (Control Talk implies that the receiver has little choice and must change. Straight Talk communicates the earnestness of your request but leaves the choice to change up to the receiver.) Stay out of Fight Talk; do not slide into Spite Talk.

6. Contract with the receiver for an appropriate time and place to ask for change.

Delivery

1. *Pre-Talk.* Briefly tell the other person what you want to talk about and how you would like him or her to participate. Watch for nonverbals that indicate a readiness to listen.

2. Use the following Speaking Skills in the squence you have chosen (See #3 above):
   - *Speak For Self.*
   - *State Your Past/Current Actions:* Own what you have done or are doing about the situation.
   - *Give Specific Sensory Data:* Document the unwanted behavior or unfulfilled expectation with specific examples you have observed.
   - *Express Thoughts:* Explain your interpretation of the behavior and its negative impact.
   - *Report Feelings:* Say what you are experiencing emotionally.
   - *Disclose Wants:*

     For Yourself (from other): Be specific in describing what the new behavior would look like. (Generally ask for small but important changes the other person is able to make.)

     For the Other: Tell what is in this for him or her. (Consider the person's gains and losses.)

     For Your Relationship: Explain how the two of you will benefit.

Copyright © 1989, Interpersonal Communication Programs, Inc., Littleton, CO

- *Take Action:* Explicitly ask for change. State what you will do to support the change. Be clear about consequences, if there are any, for no change.

3. Ask the person to summarize what you have just said (to your satisfaction).

4. Invite the other person's response to your request and incorporate any legitimate feedback he or she has about you. Be careful, however, not to be distracted from your original request.

5. If appropriate, negotiate the change. For example, agree to a quid pro quo — something-for-something trade in behavior — or some other satisfactory arrangement.

6. Gain the other's commitment to the change by developing an action plan for new behavior. (If appropriate, consider building in incentives and rewards for change).

7. Check yourself and the other person for satisfaction with the outcome and any incomplete communicycles — things left unclear or unsaid. Pay attention to congruence of yourself and the other.

8. Thank the person for his or her response and collaboration, if you are appreciative. (This will help you end on a positive note.)

9. Follow-up is crucial. Over the next few days or weeks, look for and recognize changed behavior. Give the person positive feedback when you see it. (Close the Meta-Cycle Process.) If there is no behavioral change, re-cycle, asking for and structuring the action plan.

Considerations

1. If you hesitate to ask for change, what prevents you? Is it:
   - Chance of damaging or losing the relationship? (See "Why People Stay 'Stuck' in a Relationship," pages 286-87, in CONNECTING.)
   - Fear of reprisals?
   - Lack of confidence in your awareness?
   - Fear of an emotional outburst?
   - Lack of skill in handling confrontive situations?
   - Doubt that asking will make any difference?
   - Wish to remain a "nice person" and not to stir up trouble?

2. Ask yourself, "What is in it for me and what is in this for the other person?" Confront your own fears, weighing long-term benefits, to both you and the receiver, against the short-term strain in the relationship.

2. When you encounter defensiveness — your own or the other person's — shift to Now-talk. Talk about your immediate awareness rather than pursuing what is not working.

3. Keep your focus. Do not defuse your energy with anxious chatter or distracting humor.

Copyright © 1989, Interpersonal Communication Programs, Inc., Littleton, CO

GIVING NEGATIVE FEEDBACK AND ASKING FOR CHANGE
— WORKSHEET

See "Guidelines for Giving Negative Feedback and Asking for Change ," on the previous pages.

Instructions: Think of a person who is currently doing something you want changed or stopped. (This may be a difficult situation to confront.) When you have a person and behavior in mind:

1. Fill out your Awareness Wheel and complete the items below in preparation for giving your negative feedback and asking for change.

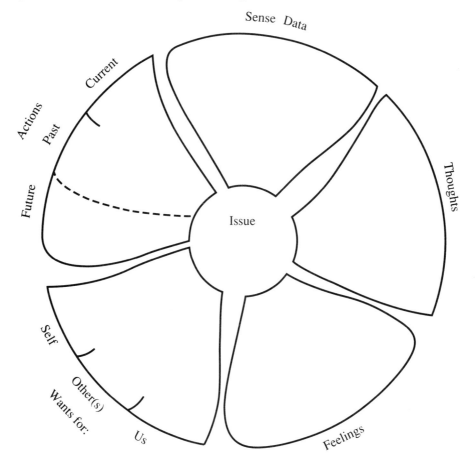

2. Think about the receiver's informational comfort zones and how to frame your message to gain the best hearing. Number the parts of your Wheel, from 1-5, in the order you think will be most effective for delivery.

3. Formulate any brief Pre-Talk message which will set the stage and enhance reception:

4. Contract with the receiver for an appropriate time and place to ask for the change.

Copyright © 1989, Interpersonal Communication Programs, Inc., Littleton, CO

ASKING FOR CHANGE — OBSERVATION WORKSHEET

Instructions: Rate the following with a mark that represents your assessment of each item. If more than one person practices asking for change during the exercise, use a different symbol to represent each person (for example: O, X, #):

		Low				High	
1.	Pre-Talked to established "contract" and gave preview	1	2	3	4	5	6
2.	Documented unwanted behavior with specific data	1	2	3	4	5	6
3.	Explained impact of behavior	1	2	3	4	5	6
4.	Shared feelings	1	2	3	4	5	6
5.	Described specific wants	1	2	3	4	5	6
6.	Asked directly for change	1	2	3	4	5	6
7.	Gained commitment to change	1	2	3	4	5	6
8.	Now-Talked	1	2	3	4	5	6
9.	Spoke clearly, directly, and concisely to the point	1	2	3	4	5	6
10.	Was respectful	1	2	3	4	5	6
11.	Was responsive to other	1	2	3	4	5	6

12. What style(s) of communication did the participants use?

13. List any communicycles left unattended:

14. What was the overall effectiveness?   1 2 3 4 5 6

Copyright © 1989, Interpersonal Communication Programs, Inc., Littleton, CO

ROLE PLAY — PREPARATION WORKSHEET

Instructions: Develop a current or typical interpersonal situation to be role-played.

1. Situation/issue:

2. Background information (context, rules, resources, constraints, what's at stake):

	Person A	Person B
3. Description of players:

    beliefs:

    feelings:

    wants:

    behaviors:

4. History of the relationship:

Copyright © 1989, Interpersonal Communication Programs, Inc., Littleton, CO

Role Play — Preparation Worksheet (Continued)

Instructions: Look over the "Connecting Skills/Concepts Menu" on the next page. Think about the situation and role you are going to play. Choose several of the skills/concepts which you would like to practice or demonstrate as you role-play.

Note: If you play the role of a "difficult" person, disregard the Connecting Skills/Concepts and play your role as the difficult person would do. However, if during the role-play, the "skill player" says or does something which touches a responsive cord in you, let yourself be influenced. If he or she does not "connect" with you, continue playing your "difficult" behaviors.

Connecting skills/concepts to practice/demonstrate:

_____

_____

_____

_____

_____

_____

AUDIO- OR VIDEO-TAPE OPTION

If you are not using this WORKBOOK in a group/class, select several skills to practice and have a conversation with someone around a real issue. Audio- or video-tape record the conversation, if possible, and monitor your skill usage when you replay the conversation. Discuss the effects of the skills you used with the other person (in a Post-Talk conversation).

Copyright © 1989, Interpersonal Communication Programs, Inc., Littleton, CO

CONNECTING SKILLS AND CONCEPTS — MENU

Instructions: Here is a list of the major communication skills and concepts from Chatpers 1-11 in CONNECTING. Choose a different skill and concept to watch during each role-play, audio- or video-tape replay/review. Use the next page to jot down specific behaviors which you see and hear that demonstrate the skill/concept.

Content/Issue:

Topic, Other, Self, Relationship

Communication Styles:

Small/Shop Talk

Control/Fight/Spite Talk

Search Talk

Straight Talk

Mixed Messages

Speaking Skills to Tell Your Story:

Speak for Self

Give Sensory Data

Express Thoughts

Tell Feelings

Disclose Wants

State Actions

Pre-Talk (contracting, previewing)

Now-Talk (observing and giving feedback, clarifying, summarizing)

Post-Talk (recounting, suggesting changes, "clearing the air")

Concepts — to Keep in Mind:

Individual Differences

Comfort Zones

Partial Awareness

Mapping Issues

Rapport/Control/Trust

Follow/Lead

Understanding Before Agreement

Hidden Agenda

Listing Skills to Hear Other's Story:

Look, Listen, Match (nonverbals, posture, style), and Track

Acknowledge Message (hot/sore/soft spots)

Invite More Information (one, two, three . . . times)

Check Out/Clarify (missing,confusing/ conflicting information)

Summarize/Share Meaning (demonstrate understanding)

Three Types of Listening:

Persuasive (to lead)

Directive (to clarify)

Attentive (to discover)

Concepts — To Watch For:

Incomplete Communicycles

Impasses

Nonverbal Incongruence

Dance Patterns

Action, Reaction, Interaction

Copyright © 1989, Interpersonal Communication Programs, Inc., Littleton, CO

CONNECTING SKILLS AND CONCEPTS
— OBSERVATION WORKSHEET

Instructions: List a different skill and concept (from the preceding page) to watch for during each role-play, audio or video replay/review.

Players' Names   _____   _____

Skill/Concept   _____   _____

Players' Names   _____   _____

Skill/Concept   _____   _____

Players' Names   _____   _____

Skill/Concept   _____   _____

Players' Names   _____   _____

Skill/Concept   _____   _____

Copyright © 1989, Interpersonal Communication Programs, Inc., Littleton, CO

FRAMEWORKS, PROCESSES, AND SKILLS — PROGRESS REVIEW

Instructions: Rate yourself by placing an "X" in the blank to indicate where you think you are in the process of learning each of the frameworks, processes, and skills presented so far in CONNECTING.

Review Dates: _____   _____

_____   _____

Applying Frameworks	Initial Awareness	Awkward Use	Conscious Use	Natural Use
Three Types of Listening				
The Meta-Cycle Process				
Facilitating Processes				
Multi-Part Statements				
Rapport, Control, Trust				
Awareness Wheel and Open Questions				
Hot, Sore, Soft Spots				
Getting to the Core				
Sharing-Meaning Process				
Noticing the Dance				
Watching Congruence/Incongruence				
Contracting: Setting Procedures				
Stories				
Using Skills				
1. Speaking for Self				
2. Giving Sensory Data				
3. Expressing Thoughts				
4. Reporting Feelings				
5. Disclosing Wants				
6. Stating Actions				

Copyright © 1989, Interpersonal Communication Programs, Inc., Littleton, CO

Progress Review (Continued)

Using Skills	Initial Awareness	Awkward Use	Conscious Use	Natural Use
7. Looking, Listening, Matching, and Tracking				
8. Acknowledging Messages				
9. Inviting Messages				
10. Checking Out/Clarifying Information				
11. Summarizing — To Ensure Accuracy of Understanding				
Pre-Talk				
Now-Talk				
Post-Talk				

Check the frameworks, processes, and skills you want particularly to practice over the next two weeks.

Copyright © 1989, Interpersonal Communication Programs, Inc., Littleton, CO

Notes

Copyright © 1989, Interpersonal Communication Programs, Inc., Littleton, CO

12

RELATIONSHIPS AS SYSTEMS

OUTLINE

Properties of Human Systems

Six characteristics comprise human systems — being purposeful, interconnected, bounded, self-monitoring, information-processing, and greater than the sum of their parts.

THE CIRCUMPLEX MODEL OF HUMAN SYSTEMS

The model shows how systems balance adaptability (change with stability) and cohesion (separateness with togetherness).

SYSTEM ADAPTABILITY

On a scale adaptability ranges from rigid (very low) to structured (low to moderate) to flexible (moderate to high) to chaotic (very high).

Five characteristics are involved in system adaptability:

Leadership — Who is in charge?

Rules/Roles — Who can do what?

Negotiation — How are decisions made?

Organization — How orderly are things?

Values — What is important?

SYSTEM COHESION

On a scale cohesion ranges from disengaged (very low) to dispersed (low to moderate) to connected (moderate to high) to enmeshed (very high).

Copyright © 1989, Interpersonal Communication Programs, Inc., Littleton, CO

Five characteristics are involved in system cohesion:

Closeness — How much involvement is there?

Support — How much backup is there?

Decision-Making — Who benefits?

Commonality — What is shared?

Unity — How is morale?

THE SYSTEMS MAP

The Systems Map combines the dimensions of adaptability and cohesion into 16 distinct types of relationship systems.

The map shows relationships as balanced, mid-range, and extreme. These relationship types parallel the designations from Chapter 1 called viable, limited, or troubled.

Consequences of System Types

Research gives support to the hypothesis that balanced systems function more adequately and productively over time than do systems at the extremes of the dimensions.

USES OF THE SYSTEMS MAP

The uses include:

Increasing Awareness and Understanding

Understanding Systemic Comfort Zones

Attending to Change

Spotting Systemic Stress

Recognizing Choices

Copyright © 1989, Interpersonal Communication Programs, Inc., Littleton, CO

COMPARING SYSTEMS — WORKSHEET

Background Reading: "Properties of Human Systems," Chapter 12, pages 219-220 in CONNECTING.

Instructions: Compare your three systems (below) by recalling and briefly recording events or sayings that illustrate each of the system properties.

System Properties	Family of Origin	Current Family/ Relationship	Work/Other Organization
Purpose:			
Interconnection:			
Boundaries:			
Self-monitoring:			
Information-processing:			
Whole greater than sum of its parts:			

Copyright © 1989, Interpersonal Communication Programs, Inc., Littleton, CO

THE SYSTEMS MAP — ADAPTABILITY QUESTIONNAIRE

Background Reading: "System Adaptability," Chapter 12, pages 222-26 in CONNECTING.

Instructions: First, answer each question by drawing a *square* around the numbers that you think best describe the system *under normal conditions*. Then draw a line connecting the squares. Repeat this process with *triangles* around the numbers that describe the system *in crises or under pressure,* and with circles for the way you *wish or desire* things to be. For each condition, sum the scores and divide by 5 for an Average Score.

YOUR FAMILY OF ORIGIN

Adaptability Dimension:		Rigid		Structured		Flexible		Chaotic		
Leadership	Dictatorial	1	2	3	4	5	6	7	8	Inept
Rules/Roles	Too Fixed	1	2	3	4	5	6	7	8	Inconsistent
Negotiation	Limited	1	2	3	4	5	6	7	8	Endless
Organization	Too Organized	1	2	3	4	5	6	7	8	Disorganized
Values	Not Open	1	2	3	4	5	6	7	8	Too Open

AVERAGE SCORES   Normal Conditions: ___   Crisis/Pressure: ___   Desired: ___

YOUR CURRENT FAMILY OR RELATIONSHIP

Adaptability Dimension:		Rigid		Structured		Flexible		Chaotic		
Leadership	Dictatorial	1	2	3	4	5	6	7	8	Inept
Rules/Roles	Too Fixed	1	2	3	4	5	6	7	8	Inconsistent
Negotiation	Limited	1	2	3	4	5	6	7	8	Endless
Organization	Too Organized	1	2	3	4	5	6	7	8	Disorganized
Values	Not Open	1	2	3	4	5	6	7	8	Too Open

AVERAGE SCORES   Normal Conditions: ___   Crisis/Pressure: ___   Desired: ___

YOUR WORK OR OTHER ORGANIZATION (Team, Church, Club, Etc.)

Adaptability Dimension:		Rigid		Structured		Flexible		Chaotic		
Leadership	Dictatorial	1	2	3	4	5	6	7	8	Inept
Rules/Roles	Too Fixed	1	2	3	4	5	6	7	8	Inconsistent
Negotiation	Limited	1	2	3	4	5	6	7	8	Endless
Organization	Too Organized	1	2	3	4	5	6	7	8	Disorganized
Values	Not Open	1	2	3	4	5	6	7	8	Too Open

AVERAGE SCORES   Normal Conditions: ___   Crisis/Pressure: ___   Desired: ___

Copyright © 1989, Interpersonal Communication Programs, Inc., Littleton, CO

THE SYSTEMS MAP — COHESION QUESTIONNAIRE

Background Reading: "System Cohesion," Chapter 12, pages 227-31 in CONNECTING.

Instructions: First, answer each question by drawing a *square* around the numbers that you think best describe the system *under normal conditions.* Then draw a line connecting the squares. Repeat this process with *triangles* around the numbers that describe the system *in crises or under pressure,* and with circles for the way you *wish or desire* things to be. For each condition, sum the scores and divide by 5 for an Average Score.

YOUR FAMILY OF ORIGIN

Cohesion Dimension:		Disengaged		Dispersed		Connected		Enmeshed	
Closeness	Not Close	1	2	3	4	5	6	7	8	Too Close
Support	None	1	2	3	4	5	6	7	8	Smothered
Decision-making	Only Individual	1	2	3	4	5	6	7	8	Only Group
Commonality	Very Little	1	2	3	4	5	6	7	8	Everything
Unity	None	1	2	3	4	5	6	7	8	Total

AVERAGE SCORE   Normal Conditions: ___   Crisis/Pressure: ___   Desired: ___

YOUR CURRENT FAMILY OR RELATIONSHIP

Cohesion Dimension:		Disengaged		Dispersed		Connected		Enmeshed	
Closeness	Not Close	1	2	3	4	5	6	7	8	Too Close
Support	None	1	2	3	4	5	6	7	8	Smothered
Decision-making	Only Individual	1	2	3	4	5	6	7	8	Only Group
Commonality	Very Little	1	2	3	4	5	6	7	8	Everything
Unity	None	1	2	3	4	5	6	7	8	Total

AVERAGE SCORE   Normal Conditions: ___   Crisis/Pressure: ___   Desired: ___

YOUR WORK OR OTHER ORGANIZATION (Team, Church, Club, Etc.)

Cohesion Dimension:		Disengaged		Dispersed		Connected		Enmeshed	
Closeness	Not Close	1	2	3	4	5	6	7	8	Too Close
Support	None	1	2	3	4	5	6	7	8	Smothered
Decision-making	Only Individual	1	2	3	4	5	6	7	8	Only Group
Commonality	Very Little	1	2	3	4	5	6	7	8	Everything
Unity	None	1	2	3	4	5	6	7	8	Total

AVERAGE SCORE   Normal Conditions: ___   Crisis/Pressure: ___   Desired: ___

Copyright © 1989, Interpersonal Communication Programs, Inc., Littleton, CO

OPTIONS FOR USING THE SYSTEMS MAP

The worksheets on the following pages of this WORKBOOK are designed to help you use The Systems Map to increase your awareness and understanding of the significant social systems — relationship networks — operating in your life.

Background Reading: "The Circumplex Model of Human Systems,"* Chapter 12, page 221, and "Uses of the Systems Map," pages 234-37, in CONNECTING.

OPTION # 1: PLOT YOUR PROFILE SCORES OF THE ADAPTABILITY AND COHESION QUESTIONNAIRES ON THE SYSTEMS MAPS

Instructions: Notice that the scales on The Systems Maps (see the following three pages) correspond with the Adaptability and Cohesion Questionnaire Scales from 1-8 (on the preceding pages). Begin with "Your Family of Origin Map" and transfer the Average Scores for Normal Conditions from the Adaptability and Cohesion Questionnaires by marking the point on the Map with a *square* at which these two scores intersect. Follow the same process with a *triangle* for Crisis/Pressure and a *circle* for desired states. When you have finished plotting Your Family Of Origin Map, transfer the corresponding scores, in similar fashion, for Your Current Family or Relationship and Work or Other Organization Maps as well.

OPTION # 2: ADD YOUR VIEW OF MEMBERS' BEHAVIOR

Instructions: If space is available, you may wish to use pentagons to add specific members' (including yourself) normal, crisis, and preferential mode of operation along the Adaptability and Cohesion axis, on each Map. Write an initial inside each pentagon to represent each member. Finally, lightly draw circles (usually elliptical) around each system's "normal zone," "crisis zone," and "preference zone."

OPTION # 3: COMPARE AND DISCUSS MAPS

Instructions: Have each group member complete the option(s) above in his or her own WORKBOOK; then compare and discuss the results.

Option #1 above is your view of the group's functioning as a whole; Option #2 is your perspective of each person's contribution, as a part of the whole. Option #3 uses each member's own data to elaborate Options #1 and #2. As you study each Map, note similarities, differences, balance, and strains. Do the Maps help you better understand any particular system or relationship issues? What changes, if any, do you want to create? How might you go about changing adaptability or cohesion? Compare your Pre-Assessment "Diagram of a Relationship Network" with the corresponding System Map. Use the space below each Map to make brief notes.

---

* See the Appendix for more information on research instruments and the practical relationship feedback tools PREPARE (for engaged couples) and ENRICH (for married couples) which are based on the Circumplex Model of Marriage and Family Systems.

Copyright © 1989, Interpersonal Communication Programs, Inc., Littleton, CO

SYSTEM MAP OF YOUR FAMILY OF ORIGIN — WORKSHEET

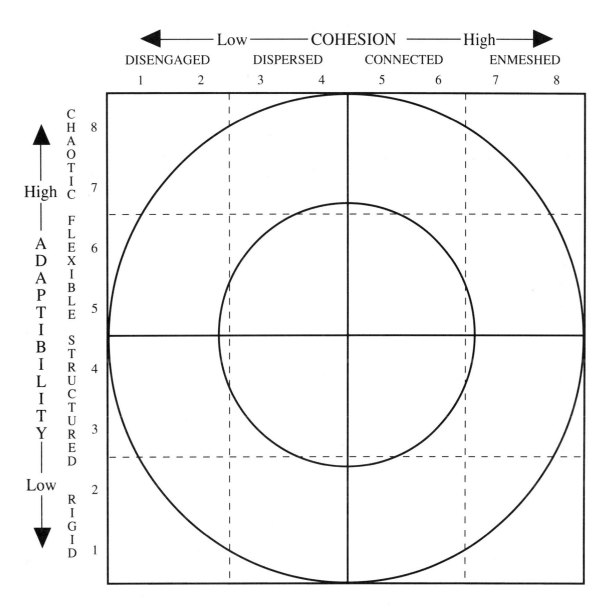

Notes:

Copyright © 1989, Interpersonal Communication Programs, Inc., Littleton, CO

SYSTEM MAP OF YOUR CURRENT FAMILY OR RELATIONSHIP
— WORKSHEET

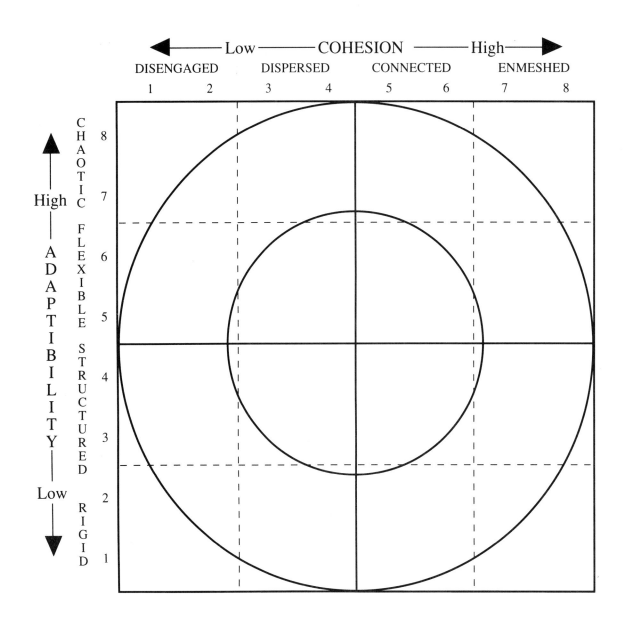

Notes:

Copyright © 1989, Interpersonal Communication Programs, Inc., Littleton, CO

SYSTEM MAP OF YOUR WORK OR OTHER ORGANIZATION
— WORKSHEET

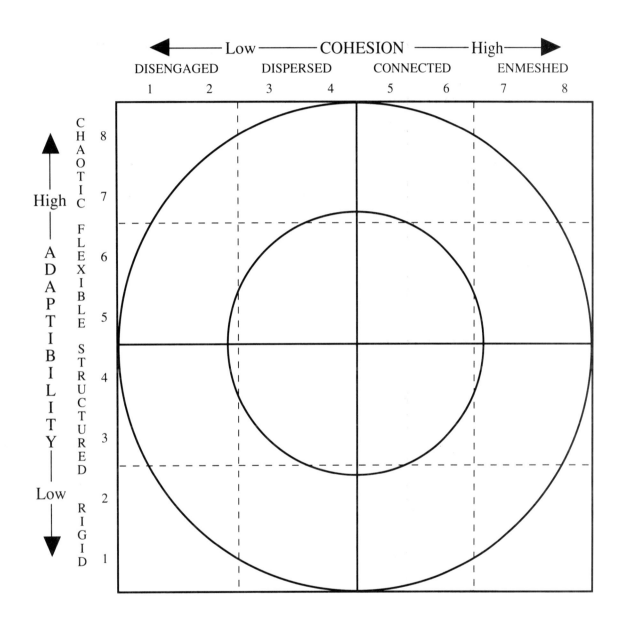

Notes:

Copyright © 1989, Interpersonal Communication Programs, Inc., Littleton, CO

Notes

Copyright © 1988, Interpersonal Communication Programs, Inc., Littleton, CO

13

RELATIONSHIP PHASES

OUTLINE

A relationship often goes through four phases across time.

VISIONARY PHASE

The imagined view of the relationship is good with the picture of a satisfying future together.

The focus is on us and our immediate future — on what we will do and be together.

On the positive side, the relationship gets off to a good start and has energy.

On the negative side, aspects that do not fit right are discounted or ignored.

ADVERSARIAL PHASE

The issues of life give rise to struggles about how to handle them.

The focus is on you and your (negative) impact on me.

On the positive side, each of us finds the means to show who we really are.

Negatively, we try to make the other person change and a poor spirit can develop. An outside alternative (for example, an affair) may be tempting.

DORMANT PHASE

Partners accept themselves and live more peacefully together.

Outsiders see a structural commitment to the relationship.

The focus is on me — upon developing my own interests (and allowing freedom for my partner to do so, too).

Copyright © 1989, Interpersonal Communication Programs, Inc., Littleton, CO

On the positive side, each person develops real individuality with relationship and emotional needs already met.

On the negative side, partners avoid issues or both go their own ways, often shutting out the other.

VITAL PHASE

High value is placed on blending as a pair, balancing similarities and differences. With real understanding and appreciation, partners make an active choice to commit energies to the relationship.

The focus is on who we are now — what we are about in the present.

On the positive side, the relationship experiences a wholeness and radiates a vitality.

On the negative side, outsiders may desire that more energy be directed to them than is available from the pair. The couple may maintain a kind of selfishness, for the sake of the relationship, about their time and energy.

Copyright © 1989, Interpersonal Communication Programs, Inc., Littleton, CO

RELATIONSHIP PHASES — WORKSHEET

Background Reading: "Relationship Phases," Chapter 13, pages 239-250 in CONNECTING.

Instructions: Pick a significant relationship in your life, such as a partnership, spouse, or friend, which you have had for a considerable amount of time. (Do not choose a parent/child relationship.)

With that person (relationship) in mind, reflect on and answer as many of the following questions as you can. (If you cannot complete all of the questions, it may be that your relationship has not experienced all of the phases.)

Visionary Phase

1. What were your visions about that person?

2. What visions do you think your partner had about you?

3. What were your visions about the two of you together?

4. What goals or dreams, if any, did you talk about together?

5. What aspect of the relationship did you ignore or discount that might have interfered with the vision coming to pass?

Adversarial Phase

1. What issues have you and your partner struggled about?

2. In what way, have any of your differences clashed?

Copyright © 1989, Interpersonal Communication Programs, Inc., Littleton, CO

Relationship Phases — Worksheet (Continued)

3. How have you tried to change the other?

4. What areas of vulnerability has your partner attacked in you?

5. What areas of vulnerability have you attacked in your partner?

6. What outside alternative has appealed to you?

Dormant Phase

1. In what areas of life have you put most energy apart from the other person?

2. Where do you think your partner has put most energy apart from you?

3. How have you developed separately that you don't talk about with your partner?

4. In what way have you let your partner go his or her own way without bothering that person?

5. What issues have you and your partner avoided because neither of you has wanted to "rock the boat?"

6. Generally, what have your feelings been about your relationship during this phase?

Copyright © 1989, Interpersonal Communication Programs, Inc., Littleton, CO

Relationship Phases — Worksheet (Continued)

Vital Phase

1. What challenge has come up that has tested your relationship strength?

2. What choices have you made, in order to commit consciously your energies to the relationship rather than to outside pressures or alternatives?

3. What choices do you believe your partner has made to commit energies consciously to the relationship rather than to outside pressures or alternatives?

4. In what ways are you both better together than each of you is alone?

5. How have you accommodated differences in your partner in a positive, supportive way that does not discount yourself?

6. In what way do you think your partner has accommodated differences in you that does not discount him or her?

Additional Questions for Reflection

1. With the relationship you answered questions about, determine what phase you are in now.

2. CONNECTING gives positive aspects that accompany each phase. What are the positive aspects about the phase you are in now?

Copyright © 1989, Interpersonal Communication Programs, Inc., Littleton, CO

Relationship Phases — Worksheet (Continued)

3. CONNECTING also gives negative aspects for each phase. What are the negative aspects about the phase you are in now?

4. How does your situation fit? Give an example.

5. How satisfied are you with the relationship in this phase?

   Low   High
    1   2   3   4   5   6

6. According to the map of phases, what comes next?

7. What phase would you like to be in?

8. If you are not in the phase you want to be in, from your reading thus far, what does it take to reach it?

9. What actions can you take to bring about the change you desire?

10. Pick one of these actions and commit to beginning it.

Copyright © 1989, Interpersonal Communication Programs, Inc., Littleton, CO

RELATIONSHIP PROCESSES

14

COMMUNICATING UNDER PRESSURE:
Reducing Interpersonal Stress

OUTLINE

WHAT CAUSES PRESSURE?

Demands, which may be real or imagined, exceed the resources available for handling them.

Three Stages of Stress
These include alarm reaction, resistance, and exhaustion.

Predictability and Control Reduce Pressure
Pressure is Communicated
Response to Pressure is More Important than Its Cause

HANDLING PRESSURE AND RESISTANCE: YOUR OWN AND OTHERS

Four Steps for Managing Your Own Pressure:
Step 1. Recognize pressure cues.
Step 2. Go to center.
Step 3. Breathe fully.
Step 4. Expand and act on your awareness.

Copyright © 1989, Interpersonal Communication Programs, Inc., Littleton, CO

DEALING WITH RESISTANCE

Wherever you find pressure — inside yourself or from others — you will find resistance.

Change Creates Resistance

Change Threatens Individual and System Comfort Zones

Comfort Zones Constrict Under Pressure

Resistance is Your Friend

"No" is the Connecting Point

Leading Rather than Following — Control is Often the Problem.

Allow the Other Person to Lead You — Invite and Follow

Agreement Versus Understanding —Your Resistance Versus My Resistance

Understanding Precedes Agreement and Action

RESPONDING TO FIGHT TALK: DIRECT PRESSURE FROM OTHERS

Apply these principles:

1. **Accept (listen non-defensively)**
2. **Blend (see the world from other person's point of view)**
3. **Redirect (ask and act toward a joint solution)**

RESPONDING TO SPITE TALK: INDIRECT PRESSURE FROM OTHERS

Apply four options:

Option 1. Describe What You See and Hear and Ask What is Wrong

Option 2. Realize that Straight Talk Begets Straight Talk

Option 3. Break State, Speak About Other, Be Silent

After Options 1, 2, and 3, Expand Choices, Map the Issue Together

Option 4. Set Limits and Define Consequences as a Last Resort

ONE PERSON CAN RELIEVE A PRESSURE SITUATION

Deal with yourself first.

Create mutual understanding as a beginning.

Let Go

Stop holding on. Let it go.

Copyright © 1989, Interpersonal Communication Programs, Inc., Littleton, CO

SOURCES OF PRESSURE — WORKSHEET

Date _____

Background Reading: "What causes Pressure?" Chapter 14, pages 253-55 in CONNECTING.

Instructions: Any relationship, material possession, event, responsibility or personal attribute can either be a *stressor* which creates pressure for you or a *resource* which reduces and overrides pressure. Rate each item below along the "stressor—resource" continuum and write the negative to positive score in the column to the right. Finally sum the scores and divide by the number of items rated for an average index of pressure in your life at this point in time.

Stressor							**Resource**		**Score**

Friends

-4	-3	-2	-1	0	+1	+2	+3	+4	_____

School/Education

| -4 | -3 | -2 | -1 | 0 | +1 | +2 | +3 | +4 | _____ |

Job/Career

| -4 | -3 | -2 | -1 | 0 | +1 | +2 | +3 | +4 | _____ |

Money/Investments

| -4 | -3 | -2 | -1 | 0 | +1 | +2 | +3 | +4 | _____ |

Health/Energy

| -4 | -3 | -2 | -1 | 0 | +1 | +2 | +3 | +4 | _____ |

Hope/Faith

| -4 | -3 | -2 | -1 | 0 | +1 | +2 | +3 | +4 | _____ |

Self-Esteem/Confidence

| -4 | -3 | -2 | -1 | 0 | +1 | +2 | +3 | +4 | _____ |

Spouse/Partner

| -4 | -3 | -2 | -1 | 0 | +1 | +2 | +3 | +4 | _____ |

Parents

| -4 | -3 | -2 | -1 | 0 | +1 | +2 | +3 | +4 | _____ |

Children

| -4 | -3 | -2 | -1 | 0 | +1 | +2 | +3 | +4 | _____ |

Power/ Control

| -4 | -3 | -2 | -1 | 0 | +1 | +2 | +3 | +4 | _____ |

Other (specify): _____

| -4 | -3 | -2 | -1 | 0 | +1 | +2 | +3 | +4 | _____ |

Other (specify): _____

| -4 | -3 | -2 | -1 | 0 | +1 | +2 | +3 | +4 | _____ |

Total: _____

Divide the total score by number of items rated for your average **Pressure Score:** _____

Copyright © 1989, Interpersonal Communication Programs, Inc., Littleton, CO

YOUR STYLE OF COMMUNICATION UNDER PRESSURE
— WORKSHEET

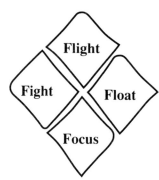

Your verbal response to interpersonal pressure is very important to your personal and relational well being. Some styles of communication increase pressure while others reduce pressure.

Background Reading: "Pressure is Communicated," Chapter 14, pages 255-56 in CONNECTING.

Instructions: When you are feeling pressure or anger, what styles of communication do you usually use? Read each of the style descriptions below and estimate your typical response pattern in percentage of time. Also list the sequence of styles you usually go through as one or two of your typical patterns. For example: joke first, then Control Talk, Fight Talk, and then Search Talk.

Current	Desired	Style of Communication Response Under Pressure
		Small Talk: see the humor and let the tension go; joke or change the subject to avoid conflict; deny or run from tension.
		Shop Talk: get busy discussing routines and details; lose the big picture.
		Control Talk: attempt to take charge by giving directions, instructions, advice; push for own point of view.
		Fight Talk: attack, blame, demand, threaten, force, abuse.
		Spite Talk: angrily withdraw; drag feet, snipe or sulk; gossip or complain; become cynical, sarcastic or defiant; retaliate or placate.
		Search Talk: try to gain an overview; consider options; suggest possible solutions.
		Straight Talk: encourage others to express thoughts, feelings, wants; candidly share own experience; commit to what can be done to improve the situation.

    100%   100%

List typical sequential pattern(s) of styles:

Copyright © 1989, Interpersonal Communication Programs, Inc., Littleton, CO

RECOGNIZING INTERNAL PRESSURE CUES — CHECKLIST

Put a check (✓) next to the items which you can use as early warning signals — internal "self-cues" — to help you **Stop** *doing what you are doing that is not working* and **Shift** *to a different, more resourceful response* to pressure.

Physical Cues:

_____ Fixed, tense, or strained eyes

_____ Shallow breathing, shortness of breath

_____ Muscle tension (possibly slight pain) in your stomach, chest, shoulder, neck, or face

_____ Fatigue

Emotional Cues:

_____ Feeling frustrated, angry, fearful, impatient, anxious, dissatisfied

_____ Feeling discouraged, stuck, blocked

_____ Losing emotional control

Mental Cues:

_____ Doubting self-worth

_____ Wanting to blame, get even with, or hurt someone/something

_____ Concentrating poorly

_____ Entertaining negative assumptions, limiting beliefs

_____ Overlooking or disregarding important information

_____ Losing flexibility/creativity

_____ Thinking only of self or other, not us

Behavioral Cues:

_____ Over/under eating

_____ Depending on alcohol/ drugs

Communication Cues:

_____ Talking rather than listening

_____ Responding reactively/defensively

_____ Pushing for agreement rather than pursuing understanding

_____ Misusing space — crowding or distancing

_____ Using Fight or Spite Talk

Copyright © 1989, Interpersonal Communication Programs, Inc., Littleton, CO

CENTERING AND BREATHING — EXERCISE

Background Reading: "Three Stages of Stress," Chapter 14, page 254, "Go to Center," page 258, and "Breathe Fully," page 259 in CONNECTING.

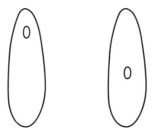

As the graphic illustrates, your "locus of energy" naturally elevates into your upper body, whenever you experience an "alarm reaction" to a stressor. Portions of your upper body muscles tighten to "resist" the stressor, creating tension in your chest, shoulder, neck or face. If this reaction does not effectively handle the challenge or threat, the muscle set is repeatedly stimulated creating strain, pain, and exhaustion. With today's fast pace, you may find your locus of energy constantly riding high in your body, taxing yourself, and others. Going to center and breathing fully provides an alternative, relaxing response to an alarm reaction.

Instructions: Have someone read the instructions below to you slowly as you practice "going to center."

- Find space in a room where you can stand comfortably. Let your eyes de-focus or close if you wish. (Pause.)

- While standing, notice any tension, tightness, and even slight pain in your stomach, chest, shoulders, neck or face. If you find a tight spot in your upper body, your "locus of energy" has been riding high near this area, accumulating stress and straining your muscles.

- Now, take a deep breath and relax. (Pause.) Take another deep breath, only this time "breathe diaphragmatically," using your diaphragm muscle (on the floor of your stomach) to expand your stomach downward and rib cage outward as you draw more air into your body. (Practice breathing diaphragmatically several times.)

- Next, gently place three fingers about one inch below your navel and press slightly. Now shift your "locus of energy" from your upper body down to your "center of gravity" — the point just below your navel — and relax as you breathe. Do not force the shift; just let it happen. It takes some practice to experience this shift to center. (Pause.)

- Now, to give you experience dropping your "locus of energy" even lower in your body, do this. Imagine that you are a mighty oak tree standing tall on a beautiful green hill. As you stand, feel the ground pressing against the bottom of your feet and visualize deep roots giving you stability as they grow out of your feet, deep

Copyright © 1989, Interpersonal Communication Programs, Inc., Littleton, CO

Centering And Breathing — Exercise (Continued)

into the soil. As the wind begins to blow, let yourself sway as you breathe fully and relax. (Pause.) Note how your locus of energy (the tree's center of gravity) has moved down around your ankles. (Pause.) Now slowly bring your energy up through your legs to your own center of gravity just below your navel. Notice how you can control your energy.

- Finally, with conscious practice you can learn to "go to center and breathe fully," instantly, in any situation — whether sitting, standing, walking, or lying down — whenever you experience an alarm reaction. This readies you to respond to stressors in more effective and non-stressful ways.

- Let your eyes open slowly.

Copyright © 1989, Interpersonal Communication Programs, Inc., Littleton, CO

MANAGING YOUR OWN ANGER/PRESSURE — GUIDELINES

1. Recognize your own pressure cues — physically, emotionally mentally, and behaviorally.

2. Re-balance yourself — go to center/breathe fully. With practice, this can be done in seconds.

3. Expand your self-awareness. Use the Awareness Wheel for Self-Talk — discover what you are really sensing, thinking, feeling, and wanting for self and others.

4. "Act on" your awareness — operate from center and use your awareness to respond effectively to your stressors. This contrasts with "acting out" — blindly striking out verbally or physically, which creates more distress for yourself and others.

5. When you speak, move beyond Fight Talk or Spite Talk.

Tips

1. Practice going to center in non-stressful situations, so that you can more readily draw on this resource during "alarm reactions."

2. Sometimes acting on your awareness allows you to see the humor in the situation and not take yourself so seriously. Enjoy a laugh, and let the pressure go.

3. Watch for your own insistence (resistance) to other's resistance (your reaction to other's action). Go to center/breathe fully.

4. Remember, your stress is often reflected in other's resistance.

Copyright © 1989, Interpersonal Communication Programs, Inc., Littleton, CO

INITIATING CHANGE: INFLUENCING OTHERS — GUIDELINES

How often have you felt surprised, frustrated, and angered when in effect you have said, "Follow me" or "Do that" (usually in Control Talk) and no one responded as you envisioned? When this happens, most of us quickly turn to Pulling or Pushing in Fight Talk to try to initiate change. (See "The Interpersonal Dance, Second and Third States," Chapter 1, pages 17-20, in CONNECTING.)

A person who can Lead and Direct others in a way that engages them in Following and Complying behaviors has positive leadership skills.

Leading by Following — A Paradox

Effective leadership begins with following — putting money in your relationship bank — before attempting to lead or direct.

Before you attempt to influence or lead another person, *connect* with him or her by:

- *Following* — looking, listening to, matching, and acknowledging the other person, until you arrive at the point at which you are:
- *Blending* — interacting (dancing in sync) unaware of who is leading or following. (See "The Interpersonal Dance, First State, Positive Togetherness," Chapter 1, page 15, in CONNECTING.)

Then:

- *Test leading* — initiate change and observe the other person's nonverbals for Following/Complying behaviors.

If the other person follows you, continue leading until you have completed the change.

If the other person does not follow you, or stops following you, recycle the connecting process (above) by following and blending with him or her again.

Interpersonal influence and leadership is not a one-act command, but rather a series of Following and Leading interactions.

Copyright © 1989, Interpersonal Communication Programs, Inc., Littleton, CO

TRANSFORMING ANOTHER'S RESISTANCE INTO A RESOURCE — GUIDELINES

1. Resistance is your "friend." It will direct you to the core of an issue that must be resolved. Defense is a natural response —an alarm reaction — to most "pinch messages" and signals (demands or requests) for change. It is communicated as reluctance, an objection, hesitation, etc.

2. Involvement and listening are major antidotes to resistance (defense).

3. When you encounter resistance, shift. Stop talking, center/breathe, and let the other person take the lead. Invite the person to tell his or her story. Let the person direct you to the central objection — the critical soft or sore spot for unlocking change. Be willing and able to leave your own comfort zone to explore and experience the other's comfort zone.

4. When you feel the urge to react — defend or attack — invite again! When you feel the urge to push, give space and choice. Mirror his or her "dance" steps.

5. Look for turning points — small but significant nonverbal and verbal increases or decreases in resistance (tightening and loosening) as you follow the other person. Keep doing what is working; stop doing what is not working! (Remember, nonverbal signs of softening preceed verbal change.)

6. After following, test leading. Ask to tell your story, or incorporate his or her concerns along with your own into a proposed action. If or when the other person stops following, recycle the process (above) until you incorporate all resistance into a negotiated action plan.

7. Resistance cannot always be reduced or eliminated. When "no" is really "no," the earlier you confirm this, the sooner you can realistically plan with this information in mind.

Tips

1. Use Pre-Talk to anticipate and disarm resistance. (See "Anticipating — Defusing and Disarming — Resistance," Chapter 11, page 211 in CONNECTING.)

2. Attend to others' wants — what's in it for them.

3. Use Now-talk to shift from the topic or issue at hand, to talking about the pattern of interaction. Comment on what you see/think is going on and acknowledge your own actions (contribution). Ask the other person what he or she sees/thinks is going on.

4. Following helps you connect (or re-connect) before you attempt to lead.

5. Persist with openness, rather than conclusions.

Copyright © 1989, Interpersonal Communication Programs, Inc., Littleton, CO

CREATING A RESOURCE BY UNDERSTANDING AND INCORPORATING ANOTHER'S RESISTANCE — STRATEGY WORKSHEET

Instructions:

1. Think about how you typically handle a particular person's resistance to your ideas or proposals that does not work well.

2. Select and develop a sequence of actions (from the suggestions below) for handling his or her resistance more productively. Jot down notes in the appropriate spaces below.

3. Rehearse your strategy by visualizing yourself in a specific situation with this person, converting his or her resistance into a resource.

Imagine you are in a discussion with this particular person and see or hear some form of resistance — "no."

Register Sensory Data (Picture A — other's state):

Center/Breathe:

Stop and Shift (what you are doing that is not working):

Now-Talk (For example, "It sounds like you are not buying what I am saying."):

Invite (Time 1). (For example, "How do you see things?"):

Acknowledge (do not react to) what the other says and Invite again (Time 2):

Summarize:

Register Sensory Data (Picture B — any change from Picture A):

Invite again (Time 3) for additional resistance-information:

   If there is more information, keep Following and Inviting (Time 4, 5. . .):

When there is no more information, test the other's readiness to follow you by leading:

- Tell your story
- Map the Issue
- Propose something which blends his or her and your wants

Register Sensory Data (Picture C — other's state). Is the other person following you? Notice if resistance has increased or decreased since Picture A and B:

Copyright © 1989, Interpersonal Communication Programs, Inc., Littleton, CO

CREATING A RESOURCE BY UNDERSTANDING AND INCORPORATING ANOTHER'S RESISTANCE — OBSERVATION WORKSHEET

Instructions: As you observe a roleplay, audio- or video-tape demonstration, briefly note what the initiator does to track and transform to the other person's resistance.

Registers Sensory Data (Picture A — other's state):

Centers/Breathes:

Stops and Shifts (what he or she is doing that is not working):

Now-Talks (For example, "It sounds like you are not buying what I am saying."):

Invites (Time 1) (For example, "How do you see things?"):

Acknowledges (does not react to) what the other says and Invites again (Time 2):

Summarizes:

Registers Sensory Data. (Picture B — any change from Picture A):

Invites again (Time 3) for additional resistance/information:

    Keeps Following and Inviting (Time 4, 5. . .) if there is more resistance:

Tests other's readiness to follow by leading (when there is no new information) by:
- Telling his or her own story
- Mapping the Issue
- Proposing something which blends his or her own wants with the other's wants

Registers Sensory Data (Picture C — other's state). Is the resister following? Notice if resistance has increased or decreased since Picture A and B:

Copyright © 1989, Interpersonal Communication Programs, Inc., Littleton, CO

RESPONDING TO FIGHT TALK: DIRECT ANGER/PRESSURE — GUIDELINES

1. Recognize other's pressure cues — body and facial tension, language, tone, pace.

2. Go to center/breathe. Let go of your own negative energy (tension, muscle strain). Relate from center.

3. *Accept* — listen non-defensively to the other's beliefs/feelings, even if you do not agree with them. Be open non-verbally and invite the other person to tell his or her full story.
   - Display Calm Nonverbals
   - Acknowledge Feelings
   - Assure
   - Invite
   - Now-Talk
   - Encourage

4. *Blend* — neutralize the attack by seeing the world from the other person's point of view. Go with the challenger's energy; offer nothing for him or her to resist.
   - Paraphrase
   - Agree
   - Admit
   - Extend
   - Credit
   - Summarize
   - Share

5. *Redirect* the challenger — lead the person into a mutual problem-solving mode.
   - Offer Choice
   - Involve
   - Specify
   - Ask for Help
   - Put Other to Work for You
   - Take Action to Meet Other's Wants

6. Look and listen for real signs of relieved pressure. Pick up on and complete any incomplete communicycles.

Tips

1. Do the unexpected — help, rather than resist.

2. Connect with the other person's fear or frustration behind the anger. Do not challenge his or her feelings with "rational" reasons.

3. Caution: if you think there is any chance an aggressor will harm you physically, keep a safe distance, protect yourself, and leave the scene if necessary.

4. Do not move too quickly into redirecting. Accept and blend well first. Do not just insincerely say, "I understand," and begin redirecting.

5. Keep centered. Your involved but non-aggressive responses will have a calming effect on the other person.

Copyright © 1989, Interpersonal Communication Programs, Inc., Littleton, CO

DIRECT PRESSURE — STRATEGY-BUILDING WORKSHEET

Instructions:

1. Think about how you typically relate to a particular person's direct anger/pressure that does not work well. Call this *Dance A — your current dance* with this person.

2. Choose a set of specific responses for *accepting, blending, and redirecting* from the options suggested below. As you select the sequence, pick responses that "fit" (will feel natural with practice) for you. Call this *Dance B — an alternative dance.*

3. Rehearse Dance B by visualizing yourself in a specific situation with this person, responding more effectively.

Recognize the challenger's pressure cues (your signal to respond with Dance B):

Go to center/breathe:

Listen to and accept the challenger's beliefs/feelings by:

____ Displaying Calm Nonverbals	____ Inviting
____ Acknowledging Feelings	____ Now-Talking
____ Assuring	____ Encouraging

Blend with the other by:

____ Paraphrasing	____ Extending	____ Sharing
____ Agreeing	____ Crediting	
____ Admitting	____ Summarizing	

Redirect the challenger into a mutual problem-solving, decision-making, or conflict-resolving mode by:

____ Offering Choice	____ Asking for Help
____ Involving	____ Putting Others to Work for You
____ Specifying	____ Taking Action to Meet Other's Wants

Attend to nonverbal turning points (signs of relieved pressure):

Copyright © 1989, Interpersonal Communication Programs, Inc., Littleton, CO

DIRECT PRESSURE — OBSERVATION WORKSHEET

Instructions: As you observe a roleplay, audio- or video-tape demonstration, briefly note what the responder does that deals effectively with the challenger's direct anger/pressure (Fight Talk):

Recognizes the challenger's pressure cues:

Goes to center/breathes:

Listens to and accepts challenger's beliefs/feelings by:

____ Displaying Calm Nonverbals	____ Inviting
____ Acknowledging Feelings	____ Now-Talking
____ Assuring	____ Encouraging

Blends with other by:

____ Paraphrasing	____ Extending	____ Sharing
____ Agreeing	____ Crediting	
____ Admitting	____ Summarizing	

Redirects the challenger into a mutual problem-solving, decision-making, or conflict-resolving mode by:

____ Offering Choice	____ Asking for Help
____ Involving	____ Putting Others to Work for Him or Her
____ Specifying	____ Taking Action to Meet Other's Wants

Attends to nonverbal turning points (signs of relieved pressure):

What, if anything, does the responder do that increases or extends the challenger's pressure?

Copyright © 1989, Interpersonal Communication Programs, Inc., Littleton, CO

RESPONDING TO SPITE TALK: PASSIVE PRESSURE/ANGER
— GUIDELINES

1. Recognize other's passive pressure cues — posture, facial expression, lack of eye contact, gestures, words, tone, or pace.

2. Go to center/breathe. Do not be intimidated by the other person's silence — anger. Relate from center.

3. Describe what you see/hear and pursue a Straight-Talk conversation. Do not let Spite Talk go unacknowledged.

4. If you do not get a straight response, and choose to pursue the negativity, decide yourself when, where, and how. (The more angry and passive the person, the more frequently he or she will deny that anything is wrong.)

5. If you choose to pursue the thoughts, feelings, and wants behind the Spite Talk, do the following:

   Break State (shift from a physical, mental, emotional *stuck state* into a more potentially *receptive state*):
   - Involve the other person in doing something which changes his or her posture. Get him or her breathing more fully.
   - Leave the immediate area together if possible. Take a walk and talk.
   - Avoid sitting and trying to talk to someone in a stuck state.

   Speak For Self About the Other Person:
   Draw the other person out by filling out what you think is in his or her Awareness Wheel — what he or she is experiencing. Watch for small nonverbal responses as you talk:
   - If you are accurate, you will see small affective changes, for example, moist eyes, slight nodding of head "yes," freer breathing, and more eye contact.
   - If you are inaccurate, it is difficult for the other person not to set you straight by telling you what is actually going on with him or her. This gets the person talking to you, moving toward connecting.

   Be Silent:

   Wait for the other person to talk. Build on small positive responses. If there is no positive response, tell the person to take his or her time to think about what you have said. Also tell him or her that unless you hear differently, you will assume your assessment is accurate. Leave the situation (non-spitefully). Let the other person initiate the next conversation. In the meanwhile, notice any positive responses and give positive feedback, if appropriate.

Copyright © 1989, Interpersonal Communication Programs, Inc., Littleton, CO

Responding to Spite Talk: Passive Pressure/Anger — Guidelines (Continued)

6. If the passive challenger shows signs of responding positively, Map the Issue together.

7. If necessary, set limits and define consequences. Sometimes the best way to handle Spite Talk and other specific passive behaviors is to tell the other person that such behavior (be specific) is unacceptable and must stop or specific consequences will follow. If the unacceptable behavior continues, follow through with the consequences.

Tip

1. Remember, people act with spite when they feel powerless and believe resentful resistance is their only alternative.

Copyright © 1989, Interpersonal Communication Programs, Inc., Littleton, CO

PASSIVE PRESSURE — STRATEGY-BUILDING WORKSHEET

Instructions:

1. Think about how you typically relate to a particular person's indirect, passive anger/pressure that does not work well. Call this *Dance A — your current dance* with this person.

2. Choose a set of specific actions for *responding* to this person more effectively from the options suggested below. As you select the sequence, pick responses that "fit" (will feel natural with practice) for you. Call this *Dance B — an alternative dance.* Make notes below.

3. Rehearse Dance B by visualizing yourself in a specific situation with this person, responding more effectively.

   Recognize the passive/indirect challenger's pressure cues (your signal to respond with Dance B):

Go to center/breathe:

Try to draw the passive challenger out with **Straight Talk**:

Break state:

Speak for self about the other (while attending to nonverbal turning points — signs of relieved pressure):

Use silence:

Map the Issue together:

Set limits and define consequences (if necessary):

Copyright © 1989, Interpersonal Communication Programs, Inc., Littleton, CO

PASSIVE PRESSURE — OBSERVATION WORKSHEET

Instructions: As you observe a roleplay, audio- or video-tape demonstration, briefly note what the responder does that deals effectively with the challenger's passive/indirect anger/pressure (Spite Talk).

Recognizes the passive/indirect challenger's pressure cues:

Goes to center/breathes:

Tries to draw the passive challenger out with Straight Talk:

Breaks state:

Speaks for self about the other (while attending to nonverbal turning points — signs of relieved pressure):

Uses silence:

Maps the Issue together:

Sets limits and defines consequences (if necessary):

What, if anything, does the responder do that increases or extends the passive challenger's pressure?

Copyright © 1989, Interpersonal Communication Programs, Inc., Littleton, CO

COMMUNICATING UNDER PRESSURE — ACTION SUMMARY

1. List the key ideas about communicating under pressure that you want to remember and use:

2. Identify the situations where you typically experience the most pressure. Then, jot down concepts and skills that you can use to help you reduce self/other pressure in each situation.

Situation(s)	**Concepts/Skills**

Copyright © 1989, Interpersonal Communication Programs, Inc., Littleton, CO

15

RESOLVING CONFLICTS:
Building Self and Other Esteem

OUTLINE

WANTS — THE HEART OF CONFLICT

Conflict is a clash of wants and the actions that reflect wants.

CONFLICT AND ESTEEM

Esteem is active respect for yourself and others, and it is important in situations of conflict.

Esteem Postures

Two self-esteem postures are Counting Self and Discounting Self.

Two other-esteem postures are Counting Other and Discounting Other.

Reflections of esteem arise particularly in three areas: your beliefs, your wants; and your actions.

FOUR RELATIONSHIP ESTEEM POSTURES
Discount Self, Discount Other — No One Counts
Count Self, Discount Other — Only I Count
Discount Self, Count Other — Only Partner Counts
Count Self, Count Other — Both Count

RULES OF RELATIONSHIP--ESTEEM CONTRACTS

The (unspoken) rules of a relationship describe who can repeatedly do what to whom, where, when, and how.

Copyright © 1989, Interpersonal Communication Programs, Inc., Littleton, CO

An esteem contract is the relationship posture (one of the four postures noted above) that you and another person develop toward each other.

Changing Mixed Contracts

A strong force for changing interaction positively is to have positive respect for yourself and the other person and to operate from awareness and centered energy.

Why People Stay "Stuck" in a Relationship

Unsatisfactory relationships almost always stem from discounting elements in the relationship-esteem contract.

PROCEDURAL CONTRACTS

Option #1:   Traditional Contract — Agreement Not to Talk

Option #2:   Transitional Contract — No Agreement to Talk or Not Talk

Option #3:   Process Contract — Agreement to Talk

RECOMMENDATIONS FOR HANDLING CONFLICT

In following the various recommendations for handling conflict (listed in Chapter 15), first be aware of your underlying intentions.

Copyright © 1989, Interpersonal Communication Programs, Inc., Littleton, CO

ESTEEM MESSAGES — WORKSHEET

Background Reading: "Conflict and Esteem" and "Counting and Discounting" Chapter 15, pages 278-82, in CONNECTING.

Instructions: Think back to situations and conversations over the past few weeks that you have had with various people. List specific examples of verbal or nonverbal messages you have sent that communicated each of the four esteem positions.

	Message	**Situation**	**Sender**	**Receiver**

I Count Me:

   1.

   2.

   3.

I Don't Count Me:

   1.

   2.

   3.

I Count You:

   1.

   2.

   3.

I Don't Count You:

   1.

   2.

   3.

Copyright © 1989, Interpersonal Communication Programs, Inc., Littleton, CO

ISSUES AND RELATIONSHIP-ESTEEM POSTURES

Background Reading: "Four Relationship-Esteem Postures," Chapter 15, pages 282,-84, in CONNECTING, and the ISSUES — CHECKLIST, pages 32 and 33 in this WORKBOOK.

Instructions: Think about your relationship with a significant person in your life. Choose a specific time period (a few weeks or months) and recall all the issues you have encountered together. As you identify an issue, list it below in one of the four Relationship-Esteem Postures that represents how you have counted or discounted self and other in dealing with the issue/situation. Then, briefly list a word or phrase which represents an exchange or event between you that documents your choice of posture. At this point, do not write anything under the column labeled, "Action Plan."

Time Period: _____ Today's Date: _____

Counting Posture	Issues/ Situations	Exchange/Event Which Documents Posture	Action Plan
I Don't Count Me/ I Don't Count You			
I Count Me/ I Don't Count You			
I Don't Count Me/ I Count You			
I Count Me/ I Count You			

Finally, under "Action Plan," jot down notes on how you will go about changing your dance (pattern of interaction) to change your counting or discounting posture around any issues you choose to change.

Copyright © 1989, Interpersonal Communication Programs, Inc., Littleton, CO

STAND IN OTHER'S SHOES — WORKSHEET

Instructions: Think of a person (at home, at work, or in another situation) with whom you are experiencing some tension. For a few minutes, become that person and fill in the Awareness Wheel below in his or her shoes.

Pay particular attention to parts which are difficult for you to fill in.

After you have experienced his or her situation as fully as possible, set aside some time to talk with the person about what you have done. Find out if you were really able to get into his or her world. Talk about what you discovered and the parts about which you were unsure.

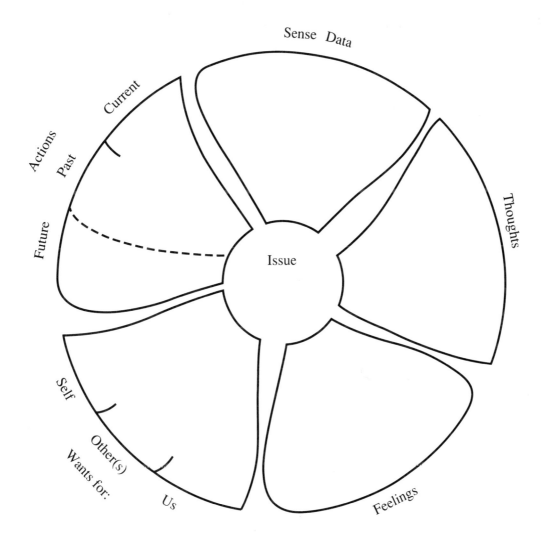

Copyright © 1989, Interpersonal Communication Programs, Inc., Littleton, CO

BASIC STRATEGIES FOR CONFLICT RESOLUTION
— STRATEGY-BUILDING WORKSHEET

Most people do not have a strategy (except to win) when they enter or find themselves in a conflict situation. However, there are a number of different ways to resolve conflicts effectively depending on the situation and the people involved. Once you become aware of the ingredients of conflict resolution, you can build and monitor your own processes (steps) for resolving conflict.

Background Reading: "Resolving Conflicts," Chapter 15, pages 277-78, "Conflict and Esteem," pages 278-84, and "Alternative Mapping Strategies," Chapter 8, page 138, in CONNECTING.

Instructions: Read over the two sample strategies A and B below. Then use the space provided (Strategy C) to build your own *basic* conflict-resolution strategy, in anticipation of tackling a specific conflict with another person or set of people in your life. Draw on the concepts and skills presented in CONNECTING to structure the process. (Write small on the lines provided to leave room for additional information to be included from the worksheet on the next page.)

STRATEGY A

Pre-Talk (preview/contract)

Identify Issue

Check Out Other's Wants

Disclose your Wants

State What You Will Do *For* the Other

State What You Would Like the Other

to Do *For* You.

STRATEGY B

Pre-Talk (preview/contract)

Identify Issue

Brainstorm Alternative Solutions

Evaluate alternative (sense, think, fee)

Choose an Action Plan

Implement Action Plan

Evaluate Outcome

STRATEGY C

_____   _____

_____   _____

_____   _____

_____   _____

Copyright © 1989, Interpersonal Communication Programs, Inc., Littleton, CO

SUB-ROUTINES FOR ENHANCING
A BASIC CONFLICT RESOLUTION STRATEGY

Background Reading: "Recommendations for Handling Conflict," Chapter 15, pages 290-94 in CONNECTING.

Instructions: Here is a check list of recommendations (sub-routines) for enhancing any basic conflict-resolution strategy you develop. Add several items to refine the basic Strategy C you developed on the previous worksheet.

___ Identify Your Intention:
control or collaborate
win or connect
count/discount

___ Consider Context of Conflict

___ Set Ground Rules

___ Figure Recent Ratio of Positive/
Negative Messages

___ Focus on Issue

___ Expand Self/Other Awareness
comfort zones
unnecessary defenses
differences as resources

___ Manage Anxiety
center/breathe

___ Deal with Feelings before Facts

___ Identify Areas of Agreement

___ Demonstrate Understanding
summarize/shared meaning

___ Express Wants *for* Other

___ Focus on *Interests* (wants) and Options
(possible actions) not Positions (who's
right/wrong, etc.)

___ Look for Common (higher order)
Principle

___ Be Specific About a Successful
Outcome

___ Avoid Superimposing Solutions

___ Determine if Everyone Receives
Benefits

___ Percent a Successful Outcome

___ Watch Nonverbals for Real Agreement

___ Know your Backup Action

___ Monitor Progress with Now-Talk

___ Monitor Internal/External Cues

___ Post-Talk to Celebrate the Solution

___ Realize *Process* Determines *Outcome*

Copyright © 1989, Interpersonal Communication Programs, Inc., Littleton, CO

DISSOLVING IMPASSES — GUIDELINES

Interpersonal impasses — rigid, polarized conflicts — can occur around any issue. The key to your dissolving an impasse is to *stop* what you are doing that is contributing to the impasse, and *do* something different — almost anything — which will loosen positions. Often an effective response is 180 degrees (in the opposite direction) from the action which is keeping you stuck.

Note: Examine your intentions and feelings in an impassse. Do you want to connect or control, build or destory? Is your desperation locking you up?

Here is a partial list of non-typical responses for disolving impasses. Invent or list a few of your own:

- Pre-Talk
- Shift Styles
- Become Least Involved (without spite), if You Are Most Involved
- Give Up the Certainty of Misery for the Uncertainty of Change
- Alter Your Dependency
- Consider Risking Loss for Gain
- Now-Talk
- Operate in Other's Comfort Zone
- Question your "Rational" Beliefs
- Determine the Level of the Real Impasse

- Genuinely Reframe a Situation (See the Situation Positively)
- Do Something *for the* Other
- Break State
- Allow Silence
- Follow Rather than Lead
- "Resistance is Your Friend": Invite, Follow, Invite, Follow, Invite
- Summarize and Wait
- Explore Missing Information/Hidden Agenda
- Allow Things to Worsen
- Make a Commitment
- Let Go
- Ask for Forgiveness
- Set Limits
- Accept the Impasse and Plan Accordingly

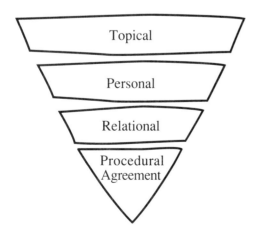

Copyright © 1989, Interpersonal Communication Programs, Inc., Littleton, CO

COUNTING/DISCOUNTING POSTURES OBSERVATION
— WORKSHEET

Background Reading: "Conflict and Esteem," "Counting and Discounting," and "Four-Relationship-Esteem Postures," Chapter 15, pages 278-84, in CONNECTING.

Instructions: Use this worksheet to record the words or phrases you hear, and the non-verbals you see which indicate counting/discounting messages as you observe role-plays, or listen to audio-video-tape recorded discussions from your Pre-Work or other sources.

	Role-Play/ Tape # 1	Role-Play/ Tape # 2	Role-Play/ Tape # 3
Discount Self/ Discount Other			
Count Self/ Discount Other			
Discount Other/ Count Self			
Count Self/ Count Other			

Copyright © 1989, Interpersonal Communication Programs, Inc., Littleton, CO

SYSTEM RULES FOR HANDLING CONFLICT — WORKSHEET

Every relationship and organization has rules for handling conflict. Some rules are *formal* and *explicitly* written as contracts and policies. The most powerful and influencial rules are *unwritten*, *implicit* and *informal* expectations about permissable behavior. These rules are mainly "caught, not taught, "from observation, side comments, and direct experience in day-to-day exchanges.

BACKGROUND READING: "Rules of Relationship — Esteem Contracts," Chapter 15, pages 285-290, and "Relationships As Systems" Chapter 12, pages 219-237, in CONNECTING.

Instructions: From what you have seen, heard, or directly experienced, what are the rules about handling conflict in each of the systems below. List *formal* and *informal* rules and use a short phrase to document an event or story which illustrates the rule. Be sure to include rules which encourage as well as discourage conflict resolution.

Rules About Conflict	**Example**
Family of Origin	
Current Family or Friendship Group	
Work Group	

In which, if any, of these systems can you openly talk about the rules?

Copyright © 1989, Interpersonal Communication Programs, Inc., Littleton, CO

16

COMMUNICATION STRATEGIES

OUTLINE

This chapter ties together the maps and skills from CONNECTING so you can create your own strategies for various situations.

CREATING STRATEGIES

The word "strategy" is used to mean a planned and monitored sequence of behaviors for achieving a desired outcome.

The test for a satisfactory outcome of a strategy is this: does everyone leave the situation feeling good about himself or herself, others involved, and the decisions made?

STRATEGIZING ON THE SPOT

This strategizing requires mastering concepts and skills associated with five major dynamics in a situation:

    I. **Context: History and Current Situation**
   II. **Content: Focus**
 III. **Contract: Esteem and Procedural Agreement**
 IV. **Communication: Skills**
  V. **Conduct: Process**

Copyright © 1989, Interpersonal Communication Programs, Inc., Littleton, CO

STRATEGIZING PRIOR TO THE SITUATION

This strategizing involves four basic steps:

Step 1. Analyze the Situation

Step 2. Develop an Action and a Contingency Plan

Step 3. Visualize/Rehearse a Successful Exchange

Step 4. Act on Your Plan

EVERYTHING IS INTERCONNECTED

Since most of the concepts and skills are interrelated, if you change one of them, you correspondingly change others also.

Copyright © 1989, Interpersonal Communication Programs, Inc., Littleton, CO

CREATING COLLABORATIVE STRATEGIES — GUIDELINES

How often do you find yourself in a situation or approach an issue without a conscious process (strategy) in mind for negotiating — working things out? If you are like most people, this is probably quite often. Without awareness or skill, many people rely on three unconscious orientations — Hard, Soft, and Rational Strategies— depending on the differences in various players' perceived or ascribed "power positions."

Hard Strategies tend to Count Self and Discount Other and begin in Control Talk, but quickly shift to Fight Talk at the first sign of any resistance. Demanding, intimidating, and using other pressure tactics are common in order to gain an objective forcefully. The greater the perceived difference in power between the influencer and the person being influenced, the more likely Hard Strategies will be used.

Soft Strategies tend to Discount Self and Count Other and are polite, pleasant, and nice in order to gain an objective. They involve elements of Small Talk and Shop Talk. They may include flattery and placating behaviors but readily turn to Spite Talk when resistance is encountered. Soft Strategies are typically used when a person is in an underdog position, with little or no perceived power.

Rational Strategies are used when power is relatively balanced and neither party has a real advantage. There is an attempt to Count Self and Count Other by being reasonable, relying heavily on Search Talk and rational arguments. Objectives are often framed around "the common good." Compromise and *quid quo pro* exchanges are proposed. When strong feelings are involved, they are down-played. But when emotions or resistance cannot be handled rationally, players typically resort to using Hard Strategies as their back-up mode, and that can easily result in an impasse.

A FOURTH ALTERNATIVE

Collaborative Strategies acknowledge power and position differences when they exist, but Count Self and Others by combining cognitive and affective information to create workable solutions to difficult situations/issues. These strategies rely on Straight Talk and Search Talk in addition to a systems perspective for negotiating satisfactory outcomes. When resistance is encountered, it is taken into account.

A Menu for constructing Collaborative Strategies, based on the concepts and skills presented in CONNECTING, is located on the following page. The Menu is built around the following five basic dynamics:

    I. *Context:* History and Current Situation

   II. *Content:* Focus

  III. *Contract:* Esteem and Procedural Agreement

  IV. *Communication:* Skills

   V. Conduct: Process

Copyright © 1989, Interpersonal Communication Programs, Inc., Littleton, CO

CONNECTING — MENU

I. CONTEXT: History and Current Situation

System Adaptability
Chaotic   Flexible
Structured   Rigid

System Cohesion
Disengaged   Connected
Dispersed   Enmeshed

Phases
Visionary   Dormant
Adversarial Vital

Individual Similarities/Differences
Comfort Zones
Sensory — Intuitive
Thinker — Feeler
Want Closure — Want Openness
Extroverted — Introverted

II. CONTENT: Focus

Issue
Topic, Other, Self,
Relationship

Awareness Wheel
Sensory Data, Thoughts
Feelings, Wants, Actions

Partial Awareness
Incomplete   Blocked
Incongruent

III. CONTRACT: Esteem and Procedural Agreement

Change Map
Pre-Talk
Preview
Setting Procedure

Self/Other-Esteem
No One Counts   Others Count
I Count   Everyone Counts

IV. COMMUNICATION: Skills

Communication Style
Small/Shop Talk
Control/Fight/Spite Talk
Search Talk
Straight Talk
Mixed Message

Speaking Skills
Speaking for Self
Giving Sensory Data
Expressing Thoughts
Reporting Feelings
Disclosing Wants (goals)
Stating Actions

MetaTalk
Pre-Talk   Post-Talk
Now-Talk

Types of Listening
Persuasive   Directive   Attentive

Listening Skills
Looking, Listening, Matching,
   &Tracking
Acknowledging
Inviting
Checking Out
Summarizing

V. CONDUCT: Process of Control, Competition, Cooperation, Collaboration to Outcome

Interpersonal Dance
Pattern
Together, Transition, Apart
Space, Energy, Time
Rapport, Control, Trust
Action, Reaction,
   Interaction
Communicycle/Impasse
Understanding/
Agreement
Stop and Shift
Self-Talk/Map Issue

Manage Pressure/Resistance
Watch Internal/External Cues
Go to Center and Breathe
   Fully
Invite/Follow/Invite Again
For *Fight Talk*: Accept,
   Blend and Redirect
For *Spite Talk*: Break State,
   Speak About Other, Be
   Slient
Expand Involvement/
   Choices
Set Limits and Define
   Consequences
Let Go

Resolve Conflict
Be aware of Intentions
Count Self and Other
Feelings Before Facts
Interests and Options Over
   Position
Wants *for* Self, Other, Us

Copyright © 1989, Interpersonal Communication Programs, Inc., Littleton, CO

STRATEGIZING ON THE SPOT — WORKSHEET
(De-Briefing a Past Experience)

Occasionally you find yourself in a situation where what you or other(s) are doing is not working well. This calls for heightened self/other awareness and communication skills both to monitor and to participate in the dance.

Background Reading: "Creating Strategies" and "Strategizing on the Spot," Chapter 16, pages 295-302, in CONNECTING.

Instructions:

1. Review the "typical two-, three-person, and small-group situations for which a strategy may be useful" on pages 296-97 in CONNECTING.

2. Think back to a recent interpersonal exchange where you and the other(s) in the situation seemed to have floundered, missed dealing with the central issue effectively, or even got stuck in an impasse of some sort.

3. Use the lines on the *left below* to recall and write down "key moments" — critical verbal and nonverbal actions during the interchange. Use the lines on the *right* to enter items from the Connecting Menu (on the previous page) that you think would have been useful strategic interventions on your part.

Key Moments in the Process	**Small, Positive Strategic Interventions**
_____	_____
	_____
_____	_____
	_____
_____	_____
	_____
_____	_____
	_____
_____	_____
	_____

Copyright © 1989, Interpersonal Communication Programs, Inc., Littleton, CO

STRATEGIZING PRIOR TO THE SITUATION — WORKSHEET

On occasion an issue or situation arises in which you have some time to anticipate your actions. The more important the issue, the more useful it is to invest in careful forethought.

Background Reading: "Strategizing Prior to the Situation," Chapter 16, pages 302-04, in CONNECTING. Review the "typical two-, three-person, and small-group situations for which a strategy may be useful" on pages 296-97 in CONNECTING.

Instructions: Complete the four basic steps outlined on this and the following pages.

Step 1. Analyze The Situation: Context and Content — Individuals and the Relationship Network:

A.   What is the issue/situation?

B.   Who is involved and what are their relationships to one another? Draw an Awareness Wheel with each person's name, positioning the Wheels to represent power and relationship by size and distance between Wheels. Draw lines to illustrate the typical flow of communication among people. Indicate whether the relationship between players is positive (+), negative (-), or neutral (✓). Next, fill out each person's Awareness Wheel from his or her perspective.

Copyright © 1989, Interpersonal Communication Programs, Inc., Littleton, CO

Strategizing Prior to the Situation — Worksheet (Continued)

C. Is there any other relevant information to be noted regarding the contextual and content aspects listed below? If so, add notes below (or to the Relationship Network Diagram on the previous page).

• System dynamics — comfort zones

• Phases of group/relationship development

• Individual similarities/differences — comfort zones, common objectives

• Incomplete, incongruent, or blocked information

D. Review your analysis and list any points that you think are important to incorporate into your strategy:

E. What specifically would a successful outcome entail (look and sound like)? List several options — from your own, the other's, and everyone's collaborative perspectives.

Copyright © 1989, Interpersonal Communication Programs, Inc., Littleton, CO

Strategizing Prior to the Situation — Worksheet (Continued)

Step 2. Develop an Action and Contingency Plan: Contract, Communication, and Conduct

    A. Assuming your strategy will involve conversation(s) with one or more individuals, in what sequence will you meet with whom, where, and when?

    B. Taking into account what you want to accomplish, use the Connecting Menu to plan a sequence of concepts and skills which you want to follow for each conversation.

Person's Name: _____	Person's Name: _____
Strategy:	**Strategy:**
_____	_____
_____	_____
_____	_____
_____	_____
_____	_____
_____	_____

As you anticipate your conversation(s), what might the other person(s) do to sidetrack, block, or knock you off center? What will cue you to the fact that you are off track (e.g. a feeling, your communication style)? From the Menu, list several things you can do regain your balance.

Contingencies:	**Contingencies:**
_____	_____
_____	_____
_____	_____
_____	_____

Step 3. Visualize/Rehearse a Successful Exchange.

    If you encounter difficulties in your visualization, consider your contingencies.

Step 4. Set a Time and Place to Act on Your Plan.

Copyright © 1989, Interpersonal Communication Programs, Inc., Littleton, CO

STRATEGY OBSERVATION/COACHING — WORKSHEET

1. As you observe each roleplay, see if you can chart the initiator's strategy. After the interchange is completed, compare your observations with the initiator's intended strategy:

Person's Name: _____   Person's Name: _____
Strategy: **Strategy:**

_____   _____

_____   _____

_____   _____

_____   _____

_____   _____

_____   _____

_____   _____

2. (Optional) Before the roleplay, write down the initiator's contingency list. As you observe, if you see the initiator getting stuck or off track, coach him or her by briefly suggesting a contingency.

Contingencies: **Contingencies:**

_____   _____

_____   _____

_____   _____

_____   _____

3. Effectiveness of Strategies:
   a. Did the initiator get to the core of the issue?   ___Yes ___? ___No
   b. Was resistance handled well?   ___Yes ___? ___No
   c. Was each person able to tell his or her story and be understood   ___Yes ___? ___No
   d. Were any communicycles left incomplete?   ___Yes ___? ___No
   e. Did the initiator maintain a We-Count mind-set: ___Yes ___? ___No
   f. Did the outcome fit all parties: ___Yes ___? ___No

Copyright © 1989, Interpersonal Communication Programs, Inc., Littleton, CO

RELATIONSHIP FRAMEWORKS AND PROCESSES
— PROGRESS REVIEW

Instructions: Rate yourself by placing an "X" in the blank to indicate where you think you are in the process of learning each of the frameworks, processes, and skills presented in the last two sections of CONNECTING.

Review Dates: _____   _____

_____   _____

Applying Frameworks	Initial Awareness	Awkward Use	Conscious Use	Natural Use
The Systems Map				
Relationship Phases				
Four Esteem Postures				
Rules of Relationship — Esteem Contracts				
Communication Strategies				
CONNECTING Menu				
Facilitating Processes				
System Dynamics				
Three Stages of Stress				
Managing Your Own Pressure				
Dealing With Resistance				
Responding to Fight Talk				
Responding to Spite Talk				
Building Self Esteem				
Building Other Esteem				
Resolving Conflicts				
Strategizing on the Spot				
Strategizing Prior to the Situation				

Check the frameworks and processes you want particularly to practice over the next two weeks.

Copyright © 1989, Interpersonal Communication Programs, Inc., Littleton, CO

POST-ASSESSMENT

POST-ASSESSMENT #1:
AN IMPORTANT-SYSTEM (RELATIONSHIP) DIAGRAM

Instructions: Review your "Current System" and "Desired System" diagrams on pages 10 and 11 in Pre-Assessment #1. in this WORKBOOK.

1. What do you understand about this system that you did not realize at the time of your Pre-Assessment? Indicate any insights you have gained:

2. Use a blank piece of paper and draw this system as you are now experiencing it.

3. Compare your "present" experience with your earlier "current" and "wish" diagrams:

4. List any changes you have made in the way you relate to people in the system:

Copyright © 1989, Interpersonal Communication Programs, Inc., Littleton, CO

POST-ASSESSMENT #2:
A SAMPLE "HUMAN CHECKERS" DECISION DANCE

Instructions: Review the decision that was in process and your "Current" and "Desired" dances at the time of your Pre-Assessment #2. (See page 12 in this WORKBOOK.)

Your Actual Dance

1. Diagram how the decision was actually decided (danced).

2. What specific steps (insights, actions, skills, or processes) went into the actual dance?

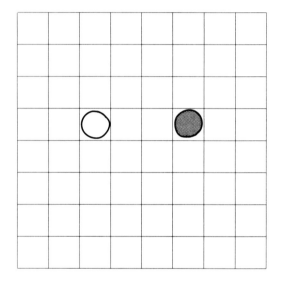

POST-ASSESSMENT #3:
AN AUDIO- OR VIDEO-TAPE SAMPLE OF
CURRENT COMMUNICATION SKILLS

Instructions:

1. Review the instructions on page 13 for Pre-Assessment #3, and make a new audio- or video-tape with the same person, if possible, of the four Discussion Tasks.

2. Use the CONNECTING MENU (see page 196) to compare the differences between your first set of Discussion Tasks and this last set. Identify specific examples which illustrate how your interpersonal communication skills have improved.

3. If you are unable to make a new tape, re-play your original Discussion Tasks and use the CONNECTING MENU to identify specific skills and processes which you could now use to enhance your discussion.

Copyright © 1989, Interpersonal Communication Programs, Inc., Littleton, CO

POST-ASSESSMENT #4:
THE CONNECTING COMMUNICATION/
RELATIONSHIP QUESTIONNAIRE

Below is the list of skills and processes taught in CONNECTING and this WORKBOOK.

Instructions:

Step 1. Mark each item twice: first with an "X" to represent your typical behavior and again with an "O" (circle) to represent your more-so or less-so desired behavior. If your typical and desired behaviors are the same, the "X" and "O" marks will be on the same number. If they are not the same, the marks will fall on different numbers.

Step 2. When you have completed marking all the items, calculate the numerical difference between typical and desired scores for each item and record the results in the "difference" column. If the "X" and "O" are on the same number, the difference = 0. If the "X" is on 5 and the "O" is on 2, the difference = 3. Note that the "O" can be located on a higher or lower number than the "X." Do not be concerned about the higher or lower direction of the scores, just calculate the numerical difference between the marks.

How often do you:

	Often	Seldom	Difference
1. Recognize your impact, positively or negatively, on others?	1 2 3	4 5 6	_____
2. Analyze interpersonal dynamics accurately?	1 2 3	4 5 6	_____
3. Attend to issues, misunderstandings, and breakdowns in communication?	1 2 3	4 5 6	_____
4. Use effective styles of communication?	1 2 3	4 5 6	_____
5. Identify blind spots and blockages in your awareness?	1 2 3	4 5 6	_____
6. Develop rapport and trust with others?	1 2 3	4 5 6	_____
7. Respond to interpersonal stress resourcefully?	1 2 3	4 5 6	_____
8. Send clear, complete and straightforward messages?	1 2 3	4 5 6	_____
9. Attend to others' nonverbal cues as an on-going cue to your own communication effectiveness?	1 2 3	4 5 6	_____
10. Help others to express their concerns accurately?	1 2 3	4 5 6	_____
11. Discover the key information in a situation?	1 2 3	4 5 6	_____
12. Prevent or resolve impasses?	1 2 3	4 5 6	_____
13. Understand and support others' personality differences?	1 2 3	4 5 6	_____
14. Turn your own and others' resistance (defensiveness) into a resource?	1 2 3	4 5 6	_____
15. Make better decisions based on full, versus partial, awareness/information?	1 2 3	4 5 6	_____
16. Give positive feedback (express appreciation) effectively?	1 2 3	4 5 6	_____
17. Receive positive feedback graciously?	1 2 3	4 5 6	_____

Copyright © 1989, Interpersonal Communication Programs, Inc., Littleton, CO

	Often	Seldom	Difference
18. Give negative feedback skillfully and tactfully?	1 2 3 4 5 6		_____
19. Receive negative feedback (criticism) constructively?	1 2 3 4 5 6		_____
20. Deal effectively with others' indirect/passive anger?	1 2 3 4 5 6		_____
21. Handle others' direct anger productively?	1 2 3 4 5 6		_____
22. Use your own anger constructively?	1 2 3 4 5 6		_____
23. Track interpersonal or group process?	1 2 3 4 5 6		_____
24. Recognize and change harmful communication/ interaction patterns?	1 2 3 4 5 6		_____
25. Create positive communication strategies for handling difficult situations?	1 2 3 4 5 6		_____
26. Count, rather than discount, yourself?	1 2 3 4 5 6		_____
27. Draw on your self-awareness?	1 2 3 4 5 6		_____
28. Get others to listen to you?	1 2 3 4 5 6		_____
29. Count, rather than discount, others?	1 2 3 4 5 6		_____
30. Understand others accurately?	1 2 3 4 5 6		_____
31. Initiate and manage change effectively?	1 2 3 4 5 6		_____
32. Resolve interpersonal conflicts and difficult matters well?	1 2 3 4 5 6		_____
33. Attend to the right time and place for certain discussions?	1 2 3 4 5 6		_____
34. Recognize sources of stress?	1 2 3 4 5 6		_____
35. Influence without being authoritarian?	1 2 3 4 5 6		_____
36. Exercise choices in relationships?	1 2 3 4 5 6		_____
37. Experience closeness with others?	1 2 3 4 5 6		_____
38. Ask for and get changes in behavior?	1 2 3 4 5 6		_____
39. Plan and negotiate collaboratively?	1 2 3 4 5 6		_____
40. Mediate disputes between others efficiently?	1 2 3 4 5 6		_____
41. Initiate relationships?	1 2 3 4 5 6		_____
42. Recognize and deal with emotions well?	1 2 3 4 5 6		_____
43. Ask for and accept help?	1 2 3 4 5 6		_____
44. Understand group (family, work-group, etc.) dynamics?	1 2 3 4 5 6		_____
45. Recognize phases of development in relationships?	1 2 3 4 5 6		_____
Total Difference Score			_____

Step 3. Compare your Pre- and Post- Assessment "Total Difference Scores." (See pages 20-22 in this WORKBOOK.) If your post-score is *lower*, you have improved your interpersonal communication skills by moving closer to your desired skill level.

Step 4. Compare specific "Difference Scores" for items of special interest to you on the Pre- and Post-Assessments.

Copyright © 1989, Interpersonal Communication Programs, Inc., Littleton, CO

POST ASSESSMENT #5:
EVALUATING ATTAINMENT OF YOUR LEARNING GOALS

Instructions: Review your Learning Goals in Pre-Assessment #5 (See page 17). Rate your accomplishments:

Goals	Surpassed	Reached	Not Reached	Future Action (If Not Reached)
1.				
2.				
3.				
4.				
5.				

With this same orientation, evaluate your other Learning Goals. Make your notes below regarding the relationships and other objectives.

Relationships to Understand Better and Improve

1.

2.

3.

Other Relevant Objectives to Achieve

1.

2.

Copyright © 1989, Interpersonal Communication Programs, Inc., Littleton, CO

REFERENCES

Blanchard, Kenneth and Spencer Johnson. *The One Minute Manager*. New York: William Morrow and Company, Inc. 1982.

Campbell, Joseph, ed. *The Portable Jung*. New York: Viking Press, 1971.

Carnes, Patrick. *Understanding Us*. Littleton, CO: Interpersonal Communication Programs, Inc., 1987.

Curran, Delores. *Stress and the Healthy Family*. Minneapolis, MN: Winston Press, 1985.

Fisher, Roger, and William Ury. *Getting To Yes*. Boston: Houghton Mifflin Co., 1981.

Hill William F. *The Hill Interaction Matrix: Scoring Manual*. Los Angeles: University of Southern California, 1961.

Karen, Robert. *Top Dog/Bottom Dog: The Hidden Dynamics of Power, Intimacy and Self-Respect*. Pinnacle paperback, 1988.

Kantor, David and William Lehr. *Inside The Family*. San Francisco: Jossey-Bass, 1975.

Laborde, Genie. *Influencing With Integrity: Management Skills for Communication and Negotiation*. Palo Alto, CA: Syntony Publishing, 1984.

McCaskey, Michael B. "The Hidden Messages Managers Send." *Harvard Business Review*, November/December, 1979: 135-148.

Miller, Sherod, Daniel Wackman, Elam Nunnally, and Carol Saline. *Straight Talk: A New Way To Get Closer To Others By Saying What You Really Mean*. New York: Signet, 1981.

Olson, David. "Empirically Unbinding The Double Bind: Review Of Research And Conceptual Reformulations." *Family Process*, vol. 1, March, 1972: 69-94.

Saposnek, Donald T. "Akido: A Model For Brief Strategic Therapy." *Family Process*, vol. 19, Sept., 1980: 227-238.

Sherwood, John and John Scherer. "A Model For Couples," In *Marriages and Families: Enrichment Through Communication*, Sage Issues 20, edited by Sherod Miller, Beverly Hills, California: Sage Publications, Inc, 1975: 13-31.

Selye, Hans. *The Stress Of Life*. San Francisco: McGraw-Hill Book Co., 1976.

Satir, Virginia. *People Making*. Palo Alto, CA: Science and Behavior Books, 1972.

Watzlawick, Paul, Janet Beavin, and Don Jackson. *Pragmatics of Human Communication*. New York: W.W. Norton and Co., 1967.

APPENDIX — RESOURCES

Chapters 2. and 10. Feedback Instruments for Assessing Couples' Current Issues and Relationship System Orientations

Prepare: for Engaged Couples
Enrich: for Married Couples — Each partner completes a questionnaire which is then computer scored to provide feedback in the following areas: leisure activities, realistic expectations (in Prepare only) marital satisfaction (in Enrich only), personality issues, communication, conflict, family and friends, children and parenting, equalitarian roles, religious orientation, financial management, sexual relationship, cohesion and adaptability.

For more information on availability and cost, contact: PREPARE/ENRICH, Inc., P.O. Box 190, Minneapolis, MN 55458 (1-800-331-1661). You may also inquire about instruments on the Systems Model for research purposes at this address.

Chapter 6. Instruments and Readings About Individual Similarities and Differences

Brain Dominance Framework

The Couples BrainMap — Two 63-item BrainMap Questionnaires — one for each partner — and one Couple BrainMap Profile. Accompanying booklet includes easy-to-understand interpretations of each partner's primary brain orientation and step-by step exercises for discovering how each person's particular brain orientation positively and negatively influences your relationship, as well as how to put your combined patterns to work for you. Self-scored.

Couples Brainmap Leader's Guide — Directions for use in educational and counseling contexts.
                          Available from Interpersonal Communication Programs, Inc.

Behavioral Styles Framework

The Personal Profile System — is a self-scored and self-interpreted instrument designed to increase awareness of your behavioral style. Everyone has developed behavioral patterns, which grow out of distinct ways of thinking, feeling and acting. By identifying and understanding your behavioral style, you can increase you personal effectiveness in a range of people situations. Originally researched and developed by John G.Geier, Ph.D., at the University of Minnesota, the *Personal Profile System* translates complicated behavioral theory into practical and personally useful information.

Available from ICP, Inc.

Psychological Types Framework

Please Understand Me: Character and Temperament Types by David Keirsey and Marilyn Bates. After describing four basic temperaments in differing aspects of life, the book portrays each of the sixteen psychological types. 1984.

Gifts Differing, by Isabel Briggs Myers. The book presents insights about how behavior reflects sixteen psychological types as determined by the Myers-Briggs Type Indicator. 1980.

Both books are available from ICP, Inc.

Myers-Briggs Type Indicator — a set of questions for discovering your "psychological type." Consulting Psychologists Press. Available from a counselor or consultant in your area who is authorized to administer it.

Chapter 10. Book, Questionnaires and Exercises on The Systems Map

Understanding Us by Patrick Carnes. This text-workbook helps you build your Family Map by exploring how your family system maintains stability and initiates change as it moves through stages of development.

Text-Workbook and Instructor Manual available from ICP, Inc.

OTHER RESOURCES FROM ICP

For more information on:

   Materials — workbooks, audio- and video-tapes, books, instructor manuals

   Program Applications — for individuals, couples, families, business and other organizations

   Names of Certified Interpersonal Communication Instructors in your area

Write or call:

Interpersonal Communication Programs, Inc.
7201 South Broadway, Littleton, CO 80122
(303) 794-1764